Crosscurrents in Quiet Water

PORTRAITS OF THE CHESAPEAKE

Crosscurrents in Quiet Water

Dan White

Photography by
Jon Naso and Marion Warren

A MOUNTAIN LION BOOK

Taylor Publishing Company
Dallas, Texas

Library of Congress Cataloging in Publication Data

White, Dan, 1957–
    Cross currents in quiet water:
portraits of the Chesapeake / Dan White.
      p.   cm.
    ''A Mountain Lion book.''
    Bibliography: p.
    ISBN 0-87833-557-9: $35.00
    1. Chesapeake Bay Region (Md. and Va.)
—Social life and customs. 2. Chesapeake Bay Region (Md. and Va.)
—Description and travel-Views. I. Title.
F187.C5W45 1987
975.5'18043—dc19   87-17780
                                      CIP

Printed in the United States of America
9 8 7 6 5 4 3 2 1

BOOK DESIGN BY LURELLE CHEVERIE

To my mother—
and in loving memory
of my father

Contents

Introduction

*T*he Chesapeake. It is first a bay, the largest inlet in the Atlantic Coastal Plain of the eastern United States, 193 miles long and ranging from three to twenty-five miles wide. It divides a finger of land known as the Delmarva Peninsula—or, more popularly, as the Eastern Shore—from the mainland. Its waters are bordered on the south by Virginia, on the north by Maryland.

The Bay is fed by twenty-three tributaries that include the James, Rappahannock, Potomac, and Patuxent rivers from the west; and the less-well-known Wicomico, Nanticoke, Choptank, and Chester rivers from the east. Its mouth, twelve miles wide, is at the southern end, flanked by Cape Charles and Cape Henry. The eastern shore of the Bay is irregular, marshy, flat, and wooded, cut by countless creeks, guts, necks, and inlets. The western shore has a straighter shoreline and higher ground with bluffs and cliffs.

The Chesapeake Bay is as much a place in the heart as it is a place on the map. It is a waterway with boats and fishermen doing what their fathers and, before them, thirteen or fourteen generations of fathers have done since the first settlement at Jamestown in 1607. It is a main route for oil tankers and cargo ships, churning south to Norfolk, or up the Bay to Baltimore and beyond, through the Chesapeake and Delaware Canal to the ports of the north and to Europe. It is a refuge for magnificent wild swans, blue herons, bald eagles, and countless ducks and geese. It is a sea of marshes, an immense nursery for fish, a region of wide-open vistas and striking sunsets, of sullen heat and sudden storms . . . and deep-rooted, complex problems. The kind of problems that occur when increasing numbers of people overtax a resource.

Possessed of a maritime history and tradition strong enough to rival those of much larger seaways, the Bay has a fierce regional identity. It is a place with a sense of place, at a time in America, and elsewhere, when that distinction is threatened by the homogenization of American culture. The Bay is struggling to retain what is unique about her people without refusing the benefits of progress.

In the name of progress, the William Preston Lane, Jr., Memorial Bridge, referred to as the Bay Bridge, was built between Annapolis and the Upper Eastern Shore in 1952. In 1964, the Chesapeake Bay Bridge-Tunnel, a 17.5-mile-long complex of bridges, man-made islands, tunnels, and trestles—a monument to man's ingenuity—was completed,

Jog Bay, Maryland

connecting the Lower Eastern Shore to the mainland. The bridges carry travelers from the major cities of the Northeast to anywhere in the Chesapeake Bay area in just four or five hours. Circumscribed within that radius are Chesapeake communities that remain a world apart from mainstream America.

The stories that follow are of a handful of people who live in the Chesapeake Bay area and must confront the forces of change. Their stories reveal the color and life of the region and the idiosyncrasies that give the Chesapeake its character. As these people work their way through the problems of adapting to limits, relinquishing some of their autonomy, some of their individuality, we see why change is so divisive in our society and why divisiveness is a far greater problem than such man-made threats as pollution. Absent still is any real partnership between the forces involved with change. It's an all-too-familiar refrain: If only government, developer, and concerned citizen could work together, the whole enterprise might move forward more intelligently,

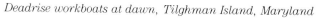

Deadrise workboats at dawn, Tilghman Island, Maryland

Produce vendor, city dock, Annapolis, Maryland

more effectively, in a manner more becoming to us as human beings, dependent as we are on natural resources for our lives.

Anyone who has ever talked with a Chesapeake waterman, or boatbuilder, or farmer, or listened to a native of one of the small towns of the Eastern Shore describe life in an earlier day; and anyone who has eaten steamed hard-shell crabs in Crisfield, Maryland, or watched a Chesapeake deadrise workboat make its way at dawn out of Ewell Harbor on Smith Island; anyone who has seen the marshes ablaze with wildflowers, or a bald eagle take wing from the top of a tree, knows the Chesapeake Bay is not only worth such a partnership, but demands such a partnership if it is to survive both as a place on the map and a place in the heart.

DAN WHITE

The Hard-Shell, Hard-Nosed, Delectable Crab

*E*arly Wednesday afternoon in mid-July, in Somers Cove on the edge of Crisfield, Maryland, and the lines of people are hundreds deep. In a field of grass and oyster shells, they stand on one foot and then the other, waiting. Their movements raise a talcum of dust that rises slowly through the warm, humid air. The sky and the water are the color of limestone. The temperature is ninety-two degrees.

Soon there will be about 4,000 people here, paying $18.50 each to come through the snow fence that surrounds the field. They have come across town from Crisfield, from up the road at Marion and Princess Anne and Rumbley and Marumsco Creek. They have come from "up-Bay," from Baltimore and Annapolis. They have come across the St. Georges bridge over the Chesapeake and Delaware Canal from New Jersey, Pennsylvania, and New York—the three states that supply most of the tourists here on the Lower Eastern Shore. They have come off the water, docking their workboats, calling it quits early, and driving over in their pickup trucks. They have come on the water in their expensive sailing boats, anchoring in the marina with their colors flying.

They have come because this event, in its eighteenth year, is the annual J. Millard Tawes Crab and Clam Bake, the biggest crab-eating blowout on the Eastern Shore, featuring the hard-nosed, hard-shell, delectable, steamed blue crab, *Callinectes sapidus*, "beautiful savory swimmer."

Two hundred twenty-five bushels of *Callinectes sapidus* are being steamed in steel caldrons at one of the seafood plants down the road. When they turn reddish-orange, they are loaded into baskets and hauled by truck to the crab booth and the lines.

Countermen hoist the baskets onto the serving table and spill crabs into piles. The hard shells click against one another as they fall and slide. The servers pile the crabs on paper plates more appropriate for hot dogs and hamburgers than for crabs. A fine orange dust settles over their arms, and over the tops of the counter and tables. Orange is the color of Old Bay Seasoning, which they scoop from bowls by the handful and fling over the crabs.

"Hey, more Old Bay Seasoning on there."

"More Old Bay? You want it, you get it. We're here to please, long as you come back next year."

Those who inhale the peppery aroma develop an Old Bay high. They experience something both deliciously salty and mind-clearing, and their sensory gratification lasts just long enough to start a craving. Then, suddenly, it is gone. In its place is a tickle, a gagging sensation, an immediate need to cough, to find something wet and cool, like beer.

"Let us know how you feel about our crabs. Come on, don't be scared. Come on, get your crabs now, get them now 'cause they'll cost you a ton tomorrow."

The people are waiting to let them know how they feel. They

Serving crabs at the J. Millard Tawes Crab and Clam Bake, Crisfield

arrive at the front of the line with whole cardboard boxes the size of small suitcases, with parts of boxes, with coolers, with pieces of board, anything on which they can carry away a load of crabs and the other bounty of the Bay: corn from the Delmarva Peninsula, steamed in its husks, stacked along a counter next to Delmarva watermelons, gaping red. There are raw clams and clams fried in strips, oysters, onion rings, and fried fish.

Behold the effort that the steamed blue crab can inspire. People stretch and contort their bodies to create new planes on which to balance their teeming plates as they weave their way to the large, striped tents where tables have been set up. The bearers of the Chesapeake bounty short-step their way through the throng, looking around en route, greeting friends, seeing who's here. They want to see the politicians from around the state that this old-style eastern Maryland happening has attracted. The politicians stand out in their tassled loafers and blazers, their straw hats and sundresses. Everywhere they go, they are preceded or followed by a claque of staff members handing out buttons and badges. The governor is here, and with him the media, their TV cameras whirring away. It's an election year, and anyone interested in public office had better have something to say about the Chesapeake Bay.

Some people never reach the tents. They stop next to trucks and cars and sit on the fenders and hoods and tailgates. They strike out for the water's edge and sit with their legs dangling over the timbered bulkhead that walls in the tons of oyster shells used to fill in an old fishing bank—one of the few firm places in this marshland where a fisherman could pull a boat onto dry land. Some eat while they walk, miraculously finding a third hand to break off claws and work out the fingers of meat. A few stand at the crab booth and eat and wait for more.

The patrons under the tents prepare to dine on tables covered with brown paper. Bluegrass music emerges from a band posted on a stage underneath two king-sized cutouts of red crabs. Conversation and laughter fill the tents.

The diners pile their crabs on the table and tuck in paper towels for bibs. They check their supply of soda or beer. Soda? "You go to Hell if you drink soda with crabs in Crisfield," says a native. "Beer is the drink here." For the price of admission, a patron of age can get all the beer he or she can drink. In this land of pleasant living, however, there is one caveat. Beer is served only in glass mugs, which are not included in the price of admission. They cost $1.50 at a separate booth. There are also wooden mallets at $1 for cracking the crab shells, and paper aprons at fifty cents to protect matching shorts and tops, or Annapolis sundresses, or blazers and cotton slacks—or whatever dress those who have never eaten crabs were advised by someone else who has never eaten crabs to wear for this extravaganza.

"I'll teach you how to eat crabs. You're supposed to whip up on these dudes."

Some of the patrons do whip up on their crabs, crushing through

the shell after the meat. Others approach the task surgically and with quiet intensity, examining every nook and cranny for the tiniest of morsels. They twist off the claws or pincers. Off come the remaining legs, and then the broad, flat shell (or carapace) that covers its organs. Out come the "mustard," the gills, the extraneous essentials. All are flicked into a heap of discarded shell fragments, detached limbs, bits and pieces of crab body, and moist clumps of Old Bay Seasoning.

At some point, all that remains of the crab is its final defense: two cartilaginous chambers that protect what the more clinically dispassionate might describe as the muscles that propel the crab's legs and back fins. But to those who endure the suffering wrought by the sharp edges of claws and shells, to the explorer after life's best and brightest experiences, the lump of backfin that pops free from each cartilaginous chamber at the touch of the knife, the very same meat that retails for $10 a pound and is fancied by Philadelphians and New Yorkers and Arabs and West Germans . . . that is the essence of seafood, the epitome of quality in taste, the incarnation of what is godly about the Chesapeake Bay.

Some like crab cold, or à la Newburg, or in quiche, or curried, or baked, or brandied, or in tarts, or stuffed in tomatoes, or any one of 101 different ways. Most people here today just like them steamed and hot, sprinkled with Old Bay, and dipped into vinegar to cut the richness of the meat.

It is the sinful greed of both man and crab that has gotten the blue crab into this predicament. At a price of $18 to $25 a bushel, a hardworking waterman out by 4:30 a.m., with 450 crabpots to tend, can earn $400 or $500 a day—$3,000 in a six-day week. That's based on early-season prices—when the world is clamoring for crabs that have not yet returned in large enough numbers from winter hibernation in deeper waters. By midsummer, crabs will be everywhere, and the price will drop.

The prospect of good money lures lots of part-time crabbers onto the water. Auto mechanics take their vacations crabbing. Schoolboys go crabbing early in the morning, or forget about school altogether. Tourists crowd the docks and piers to dangle strings baited with chicken pieces. Watermen drop their baited wire-mesh pots in all the rivers and creeks and guts and thoroughfares of nearby Tangier and Pocomoke sounds. Their faded floats are an essential feature of the watery terrain around Crisfield, as are the weathered faces of the watermen who catch them.

As for the greed of crabs, *Callinectes sapidus* has never let concern for his own cephalothorax interfere with the prospect of a good meal. The alewives used to bait the traps, the rancid chicken parts tourists tie on strings, the rotting flesh of any creature in the sea, and even his very much alive, smaller brothers and sisters (particularly the disabled ones), are all main menu items. It is easy for the crab to swim through the oval entrance to the crabpot designed just for his flat carapace. He may

bump into something stiff and unyielding en route, but his early warning system is mismatched against his desire to eat. Once he reaches the bait, he pulls at it, even though he can never get it entirely free of its wire container. After he's eaten, he meets with the frustration of being unable to find the way out, of hitting the walls of wire, and of being distracted by other crabs clutching at him. If he's small enough, very small, he can escape the way he came in, or perhaps go out through a ring designed to allow undersize crabs to escape. If he is bigger, however, his fate is sealed. He may seek temporary refuge by escaping through a hole into an upstairs chamber, away from the crowd, but that means he is two holes removed from freedom. There are three ways to enter

Shadyside, Maryland

a crabpot. The surest way to leave it is to fall out when the waterman unhooks the trap and shakes it.

Lee Wilson isn't at the Tawes Crab and Clam Bake and couldn't care less about it—he's on the water and has been there since four in the morning, as he is every morning except Sunday. A waterman, he makes a good living by working at every opportunity and by covering more ground than most of the others. He keeps his boat in Little Boat Harbor on the Little Annemessex River in Crisfield, and he drives down from Marion in his pickup truck, stopping at a diner for a sweet roll and a cup of coffee and any news about who's catching crabs where. When he pulls up outside his fishing shack, the only sounds in the harbor are the lapping of the waves and the groaning of boats as they strain against their ropes, indignant at not being trusted to go off silently and find their way to open water. The mercury vapor lights around the harbor give the white boats an eerie, luminescent quality.

Little Boat Harbor is a commercial fisherman's harbor with rough-hewn docks of weathered planks, some of them broken or missing altogether. They remain that way until passage becomes next to impossible, and then they are patched quickly without regard for appearance. The fishing shanties are ramshackle plywood affairs like the ones kids throw together in the woods without concern for perpendicular angles. The boats are rusty and littered with the refuse of fishing. A pair of old work gloves lies on a dock beside an empty crab trap. Stacks of baskets for sorting and holding the crabs await loading aboard the boats.

A boat glides by, its engine sputtering with an early morning cough. A single red light is visible in the pilothouse. Shadowy figures stand huddled together near the stern. A phosphorescent wake trembles and disappears quickly in the darkness. At his fishing shack Wilson meets his crew—his nephews Matt and Jerry, high-school-aged boys working for the summer, their eyes heavy with sleep. They load tubs of frozen alewives onto Wilson's boat, a forty-two-foot deadrise workboat named *Pa Lodgie*, after his father Elijah, a family name that both Lee and his five-month-old son also have acquired, but one that tradition has changed to ''Lodgie.'' When Lee was a boy, his father called him ''Bunky Boy'' and named his boat *Bunky Boy*. When Lee purchased his wooden boat at Deltaville, Virginia, eight years ago, he returned the compliment. The *Pa Lodgie* is twenty floorboards wide, with a rounded stern for handling in rough water. Boats ''up the Bay'' tend to be narrower and flatter, built to work the rivers and shallower water. An ''up-the-Bay boat'' has about half as much vee in it. ''It doesn't roll as much,'' says Wilson. ''It's not as quick and it lays its side to the sea better.''

Wilson switches on the engine and backs out the boat. Matt bunks down in the forward compartment to nap while Wilson heads down the

Overleaf: *Crab shanty at dawn, Jenkins Creek, Maryland*

Little Annemessex River, through Broad Creek, and over to Pocomoke Sound, where he will begin his run, pulling 450 pots, about 100 more than the average waterman.

Wilson's father insisted that all of his children get a college education because he was unsure how much longer the water would provide them a livelihood. He himself had been a waterman all his life. Now he takes out fishing parties in the summer, hunts in the winter, and makes violins, guitars, and decoys for grandchildren and friends. But, at age seventy-three, he still helps Lee, who is thirty-three, and his brother, Todd, twenty-eight, both of whom own their own boats. For about six weeks each spring, there is "right much work"—they are crabbing for "peelers," which have to be watched in the shedding trays twenty-four hours a day and removed before their shells harden.

Wilson followed his father's wishes and graduated from the University of Maryland with a degree in accounting in 1976, but he couldn't wait to get out of College Park and back on the water, where he'd been since he was a kid.

"I like being outside," says Wilson, "not being penned up behind a desk. On the water, you're your own boss. You're free from a lot of rinky-dink stuff; you ain't got everybody tugging at you, no telephones ringing. You do your job and that's all you gotta do. You ain't got as much mental stress as other jobs." His wife, Leslie, says that whenever bad weather keeps him home for more than a day, he suffers from acute mental stress and causes it too. He feels headachy, restless, and irritable. Wilson once did some accounting for a friend during a freeze-up, when the river had ice on it and he couldn't get his boat out. He got progressively more irritable sitting at a desk, until finally he couldn't stand it anymore and gave the work back. Even the normal vagaries of weather—which might keep him home only about eight to ten days a year—drive him close to distraction, and Leslie as well, since he invariably becomes an expert on how she should organize the household and care for their two children. She abides his stress with love and humor and waits for the thaw.

Blond and fair skinned, Wilson wears a baseball cap and works under an awning on his boat. But the sun has its way, and his skin generally is red throughout the summer. The breeze ripples the blue awning as he steers through the neck of the harbor into the Little Annemessex River. To the east, the sky has taken on a burnished look with the first light of dawn.

The narrow confines of the river give way gradually to open water. Small islands pass by, dark and indistinct shapes in the colorless light. The whole world is gray and flat. Only the noise of the engine and the occasional muffled remarks of those aboard the *Pa Lodgie* bring society to the solitude of open water.

Wilson has switched on his Loran, his electronic position finder in

Lee Wilson aboard the Pa Lodgie *in Pocomoke Sound, Maryland*

Navigational buoy at the mouth of the Choptank River, Maryland

which are entered the exact coordinates of the first of his crabpots. With Loran, he can quit potting at trap #289 and come back the next day right to trap #290. His boat also has radar, a depth finder, and a radio. Before Loran and radar, watermen had to know the weather backward and forward. Old-timers lost in thick weather would let out a stern rope to see if they were turning. Tangiermen trapped by fog and wanting to get home ran their boats for an allotted amount of time along a course they'd plotted on a sunny day. When they had traveled the prescribed time and distance, they cut the motor and listened for the foghorn on a channel marker. If they didn't hear the horn, they were lost. Only old-timers can do that now. Ninety percent of the watermen rely on electronic gear and would be lost without it.

Just before sunrise, the familiar sticks marking oyster beds become visible, and, almost at the same time, the first of innumerable crab floats, many of them resembling World War I hand grenades. Others are plastic milk containers splashed with paint for identification. Their presence and the sudden slowing of the boat signal that the *Pa Lodgie* has entered Pocomoke Sound, the pan-flat body of water south of Crisfield whose surface is mined with crab floats. Wilson moves his boat much more deliberately inside the Sound, his eyes peeled for sandbars and submerged mudflats. When workers from the Maryland Department of Natural Resources (DNR) drive piling for markers into the bottom of Pocomoke Sound, they sometimes need a hundred feet of pipe to reach the bottom of the mud. The Sound is a big puddle. Water depth varies from a matter of inches to just under ten feet. In the winter, ice thickness can reach three feet. When the wind blows out of the west and the current in the Sound is moving east, in the opposite direction, the sea gets very confused. There is nowhere for the water to go in the shallow, rimmed basin—except higher. In a deep, open ocean, the changes of depth are more gradual, so the swells tend to be more regular. In the Sound, and in most of the Bay itself (especially the Upper Bay), the depth changes irregularly and drastically. It shelves off from a range of forty to ninety feet in the main shipping channel west of Tangier Sound, to less than six feet a quarter-mile away. Waves are unable to form a consistent swell, and the result is what the Coast Guard calls ''a confused chop''—and what the watermen know can beat a boat to death.

There are a lot of groundings and overdue reports in Pocomoke Sound, especially ones involving deep-keeled sailboats. When people unfamiliar with the Sound don't know where they are, they tend to work their way up the myriad rivers, creeks, and guts that empty into the Sound and seem at first to offer a way out. Night traffic through the Sound is at risk, unless a boat creeps along and shines a searchlight ahead. To complicate matters further, sandbars, crabpots, and buoys have a way of changing location, and not always as the result of natural occurrences. The Maryland-Virginia state line runs through the Sound. Each state has different licenses, and different regulations concerning commercial fishing. Those differences mean nothing if Maryland watermen discover that crabs are biting in Virginia. They are not above temporarily annexing sections of Virginia by dragging the state-line buoy marker a few hundred feet closer to Richmond. And Virginia watermen will return the favor. It's an age-old lack of respect that in the early history of the country occasionally erupted into miniature wars among the fishermen.

Sometimes buoys will disappear altogether. The Maryland DNR, which polices the state's waterways, will discover them below the water, weighted by something expedient, such as an old transmission or an extra anchor, or, in one case, a pair of blue jeans, the legs of which had been tied and filled with cement. The buoys also make irresistible

targets for passersby and passers overhead. The U.S. Navy jets that streak across the sky—and are as much a feature of the modern Bay as seagulls—have been known to strafe them. Osprey tend to nest on top of the markers, and their caches of sticks often obscure the lights or otherwise foul the markers, but they are protected by federal law and cannot be removed except by federal officials. Chesapeake buoys, channel markers, and county-line markers lead a difficult life because they are symbols of regulation, reminders of DNR and Coast Guard authority over the modern waterman.

The digital readings on Wilson's Loran indicate that he is approaching his first string of pots. Wilson leaves the cabin to run the boat from the aft helm on the starboard side, two-thirds of the way back. Matt has roused himself and, with Jerry, has taken his station near Wilson. Jerry pries at the blocks of alewives with a crowbar. The skipper stands at the wheel. Within easy reach on the starboard washboard is the pothook, a long pole for snaring the rope that leads from the float to the crabpot below. Behind Wilson is a metal bin or dump box. Sternside of the engine box, on top of which are the tubs of baitfish, is the exhaust pipe running up through the awning. Only a couple of feet away from where the crew work, it is red hot to the touch, a peril in a rocking boat.

Dozens of empty crabpots made out of chicken wire are stacked on the platform at the rear of the boat. They have been drying in Wilson's yard at home. If the traps are left on the bottom indefinitely, they become coated with mud. Then grass begins to grow and eventually splits the sides of the traps. Wilson rotates his traps, pulling them out of the water every ten to twelve days to let them dry overnight so the mud will cake and fall off, taking with it any grass seeds and roots. He could also dip the traps in a chemical cleaning solution, but that would cost upward of a dollar a trap.

Wilson approaches the first of his floats and reverses the propeller to brake the boat. He maneuvers the boat with one hand; with the other, he reaches out with the pothook and catches the submerged line that tethers the float to the pot. In one deft motion, he brings in the line and loops it around a winch that he flicks on. In a few seconds, the trap breaks water alongside the boat. Water streams off its edges. Wilson reaches down with a gloved hand, lifts the trap onto the washboard, and opens a Tupperware cap that covers its bait cup.

As the water pours off, there is wild, frantic movement in the trap. Half a dozen crabs scramble along the restraining walls of their cage and snatch with their claws at whatever unseen force turns them head over claws. Matt unfastens one side of the trap and dumps it into the metal bin, shaking it vigorously to dislodge crabs hooked onto the sides. Later in the summer, shaking the traps will pose as much risk for the crabman as for the crab, for by then the Bay will be filled with sea nettles—small, gossamer bodies that resemble wet Kleenex but inflict a painful sting. The sea nettle has the distinction, along with the DNR, of being the part of the Bay that watermen would most like to be rid of. The nettles

get caught on the traps and come apart when they are shaken. Bits and pieces fly left and right. Wilson has caught a nettle in the eye a couple of times, and he carries medicine to soothe such injuries. Even so, a nettle in the eye, he just turns the boat for home and wishes he had a gun to shoot himself.

As soon as the trap is empty, Jerry stuffs a handful of fish into the bait cup and secures the cap. Wilson unwinds the line from the winch and drops the trap back into the water. He guns the boat, stern away from the trap, toward the next float, taking an angle to keep the line away from his propeller. He has had to go over the side in many a rough water to unwind an errant line.

The entire operation takes little more than a minute. As soon as each crewman finishes his task with the trap, he turns to the dump box, where a small-scale war is in progress as the crabs grab at each other and at the gloved hands of the crew, who have quickly begun to sort them.

Every now and then Jerry and Matt holler and curse as they jerk their hands back. They grab the offending crabs and fling them into the basket. Sometimes, one of them picks up a string of crabs, each clutching the other, and, if they are all the same sex, drops them into a basket. The crabs go in fighting, clutching, and in some cases still eating pieces of the baitfish, or each other. In a jiffy, the dump box is empty and ready to receive the contents of the next trap.

Females—distinguished by their red claws and their wider, flatter abdomen, which has an apronlike structure resembling the Capitol dome —are dropped into one basket. The cerulean blue clawed males, or Jimmys, which are more popular in the marketplace, go into another. "Peelers" go into yet another basket. The peeler is a crab that, in preparing to molt or discard its shell for a roomier accommodation, develops a soft shell beneath its harder one. The exchange of body armor occurs twenty or twenty-one times over the three-year lifetime of the average crab. Peelers have to be checked every four or five hours, because once they shed their old carapace, the soft one hardens very quickly if the crab remains in water. Soft-shell crabs are refrigerated until they are ready for eating. Eaten in their entirety, they are considered a time-proven delicacy, one favored especially by those who prefer not to pick through the anatomy of the hard-shell crab.

The minimum allowable size for a male crab is five inches from point to point on its carapace and 3½ inches for peelers. There is no minimum for females. Any crabs with suspect measurements are checked, and they are thrown back if wanting. A gun-toting, uniformed DNR marine policeman may be at dockside to be sure the crabs are large enough to keep. A wrong-sized crab can earn a waterman a $100 fine.

Each time Wilson nears the shore, greenhead flies buzz about the crew. Seagulls trail behind and dive for morsels of fish that fall off the

Waterman, Cape Charles, Virginia

boat or off the traps. There is a slight chop, and the pothook is indispensable. Each trap brings forth more offerings from the Bay: crabs, flounder, bluefish, sea robins, mud and grass. When the crew shakes the traps, the mud flies off, and the floor of the boat soon is as slippery as ice. It is a challenge to remain standing and away from the exhaust pipe, but Wilson's nephews are surefooted sailors and seem not to notice how close to the pipe they come on occasion.

By midmorning, the sun bakes the boat, and the crew has begun liberating sodas from a small cooler, guzzling them down between runs. The floor and their oilskin coveralls are well greased with the dark muck and with the scales and slime from the baitfish. The chop has subsided, and the sea is as smooth as glass. Each of the traps is yielding about six crabs, most of them keepers. It's not a great catch, but at least the task of lifting the traps is less of a strain on the crew's backs. By the end of the day, even with a reduced load, their backs will be tired, their clothes covered with muck, and their fingers sore from being pinched.

As each trap comes up, there is always the anticipation of finding the cage crowded with keepers, or with unusually large crabs. Wilson once found a crab that measured 8¾ inches, a whopper. Otherwise, there is little drama in the business of crabbing, and what there is soon gives way to the boredom of lifting trap after trap, all of whose inhabitants are enormously bad-tempered at the idea of coming aboard the *Pa Lodgie*.

As each bushel basket fills, one of the crew lids it, squeezing it down with his knee. Wilson likes his baskets bursting full to compensate for any settling. Each one should weigh in the neighborhood of forty-five pounds. Wilson is hoping for a price of at least $18 per basket. By noon, he has pulled 450 pots and can count twenty-seven bushels of crabs, a fair day. He turns his boat northwest and heads for home.

On the backstretch of his day's work, he relaxes a little. "You have good times and bad times," he says. "In the winter, there is the ice, maybe no income for a month. You have to put away money for leaner times." He crabs every day until the middle of September, when he railroads his boat, paints it, and puts on his oyster tongs. Fall is his favorite time of the year, and he prefers oystering to crabbing, although he prefers eating crabs. "I don't know why I like oystering better," Wilson says. "It's like the difference between chocolate and vanilla ice cream." He oysters through the winter, sometimes leaving home for a week to go up the Bay, depending on where the oysters are being caught. If he has to stay away overnight, he sleeps on his boat. If he can't find oysters, he may turn to crab dredging, driving his boat south to Cape Charles. About income tax time, he drydocks the boat again, paints it, and returns to crabbing. He works hard. What he won't say

Above: *Hand tonging for oysters off Kent Island*

Left: *Oyster dredging on the Choptank River*

about himself, his father-in-law, Grant Lawson, will. He calls him "a barn burner" and says Lee has earned as much as $60,000 to $70,000 in a year.

"It's when he's crab dredging at Cape Charles with all those big ships around that I have worried, especially when he didn't have radar," says Leslie. "Otherwise, I grew up with it. It doesn't bother me. I don't worry when he's away, as long as I get my Wednesday-night phone call from him." Leslie's father was a Crisfield waterman. Leslie, a licensed wire operator for a brokerage firm in Salisbury, was working on her broker's license, but now she is on a leave of absence while raising their two small children.

The Saturday they were married seven years ago, Wilson went potting that morning. After the wedding, they drove to the Pocono Mountains in Pennsylvania and returned on Monday in time for him to check his boat. He went back to work the next day. The first year they were married, Leslie had an oyster tonger's license and worked alongside her husband, sitting on top of the engine box culling oysters. She loves to fish. She stipulates that Sundays be family days. Otherwise, the

Deal Island, Maryland

During a freeze-up on the Eastern Shore

routine is the same, week after week. She rises with Lee each morning
and opens one eye to pack his lunch and kiss him good-bye. When he
returns at the end of the day, he sits in his favorite chair, watches the
"late news" at 7 p.m., and goes to sleep, waking up before 9 p.m. to
go to bed. He and Leslie have taken two long weekends since their
honeymoon. That means a Saturday and a Sunday. They once went to
Washington, D.C., on a Saturday and came home the next day. Wilson
does not get paid for long weekends and holidays, for staying home.
He works the Fourth of July and Thanksgiving and stays home only
on Christmas and New Year's Day—because oyster buyers stay home.
A freeze-in is the wolf at their door. When it comes to money, they are
as tight as the pine staves in a boat. Wilson owns his boat and rigging
outright, expecting the boat with proper care to last twenty-five years.
If he had to buy a new boat today, with all the technology he has
aboard, it would cost anywhere from $50,000 to $75,000.

    Time off the water may be an irritable time for Wilson, but it
isn't lost time. He spends it working on his crabpots, putting in staples,
straightening the buoys, tinkering with his boat. As vice president of the

Deal Island

Somerset County Waterman's Association, he works to influence legislation that affects his livelihood on the water.

The *Pa Lodgie* enters the Little Annemessex River and moves past the entrance to Crisfield. A steady procession of workboats is heading toward the crab factories on the edge of the harbor. Wilson will deliver his crabs at dockside to a wholesaler in a refrigerated truck who will pay him cash on the basket. The captain will wash the deck of his boat, prepare it for the next day, grab a sandwich, and head home to work on some pots until dinnertime. Over the long term, he plans to fish until he wears out, but he'd like to become more independent of the wholesaler and sell directly to the retailer. That's assuming the industry survives. Like many watermen, Wilson blames the Upper Bay for the problems of pollution but admits he doesn't know what the solution is. "Watermen didn't used to worry about pollution," he says. "We have to advance in our knowledge and technique. We don't want the industry to be taken over by conglomerates and become hired hands. We want to remain independent."

With the floors of Pocomoke Sound and much of the Bay polluted with pots, it is a wonder any crabs remain. In fact, the blue crab has become the chief cash crop for Chesapeake fishermen. More than 10,000 commercial crab licenses were issued in 1986 in Maryland, the largest producer of crabs in the country. Maryland and Virginia together

Smith Island

harvested about 90 million pounds of crabs last year. That accounts for at least half of the entire country's catch of the blue crab, which in turn is half the annual harvest in this country of all crabs (Alaskan king, stone, rock, Jonah, Dungeness, and snow crabs). Both states supplied about four million pounds of soft crabs last year, about ninety-eight percent of the total national production. Those figures do not include sport crabbing, which is thought to equal anywhere from ten to twenty-five percent of the commercial harvest.

It doesn't seem possible that a single species could be so fiercely hunted without disastrous effects on its ability to reproduce and survive. Yet the blue crab appears to be thriving, in part because it seems to have some natural advantages. It passes its critical larval stage in the relatively clean waters of the Bay's mouth. Many of the species suffering most from the Bay's problems are those that spawn near shore and in smaller bodies of water, closer to the influence of sewage, power plants, and farm runoff. The crab eats just about anything and goes just about anywhere it wants. It will even leave the water for several hours to avoid the summertime decreases in the water's dissolved oxygen. This occurs more frequently in heavily polluted waters. There is evidence also that the crab has its own built-in detoxifier; even crabs living in Baltimore Harbor, generally considered to be the most polluted body of water in the Bay, do not seem to accumulate extraordinary levels of toxic chemicals.

About the only thing the crabs are not impervious to—besides the temptations of the baited traps—is the reality of the caldrons in which they are steamed alive.

As the boats discharge their cargo at the seafood factories, dockboys dump the bushel baskets directly into large steel bins. Although the crabs seem traumatized by the shock of having been in the sun on an open boat, they are dissemblers of the first order. As they are emptied from the bushel baskets, they come to life in one last, desperate attempt to escape. Some of them dart out of the basket just as the lid is lifted, or—if they are near the top of a full bin—streak across the bodies of their fellow prisoners and drop over the edge. They land on the dock and immediately assume a fighting position, dancing back on their hind legs, claws over their heads, moving sideways at high speed. A few, a lucky few, find the dock's drain holes that open to the water below and fall to freedom. Others may feel secure in a corner of the dock with a good wall at their back, but they are likely to die there, dehydrated by the sun. Or one of the dockboys, annoyed by the crab's escape, will grind his heavy boot into it, or pick it up with his gloved hand and hurl it against the cinderblock wall. It seems that dockhands and watermen like crabs best when they are steamed or in cakes.

The large steel bins are hoisted on dollies and delivered to a caldron, where the crabs are steamed in a matter of minutes, surrendering their

Preparing to steam crabs, Popes Creek, Maryland

natural bluish-green for the more reassuring, sanitized red-orange color. Once they are cooked, they are left to cool until they can be handled. Then they are delivered to the crab-picking machine or to the pickers. The machine is a fiendish cousin of the trap, a discombobulated device that, while it mauls most of the meat out of the crab, is not intelligent enough to differentiate among types of meat, to separate backfin from the rest. The machine also requires the help of lots of human fingers to pick through the discards for meat. As noisy as it is efficient, the machine generates such great heat that it is difficult to operate for very long in the summer. It does have the virtue of washing winter crabs dredged out of the mud, a chore that otherwise would be elaborate and time consuming.

At Carson's Seafood Plant in Crisfield, the crab pickers sit in a single room at metal tables in old straightbacked metal school chairs— complete with compartments underneath for book storage. At each table are six pickers, all dressed in plastic caps and aprons, all ladies, all black, many of them related to one another: mother and daughter, sister and sister. Overhead fans circulate the warm air, and with it the conversation, the banter, the occasional laughter, the background music of a radio, the drone of flies against the small, screened windows. The piles of crabs on the tables seldom diminish. Even the slightest indentation is immediately covered over with another shovelful of crabs delivered by a man whose job it is to keep them piled high.

Zip, zip, zip. The crab is unhinged with a surgically sharp stainless-steel paring knife whose shank fits snugly into the hand of the picker. One of Carson's pickers, Tarpathia Miles, has won the picking contest in Crisfield's National Crab Derby, held on Labor Day weekend, for seven years straight. Another, Wanda Whithington, a neighbor of Lee Wilson's from Marion, has picked at Carson's for close to twenty-five years, starting when she was eleven, and her fingers are so nimble she can do fourteen gallons a day—seventy pounds of crab. Twenty-five years of picking crabs, however, is only a quarter of a century. Adeline Trantham has spent half a century, plus nine years, picking crabs. The pickers receive about $1.50 a pound and average twenty-five to thirty pounds before they quit in midafternoon. By the end of a typical day, they will lift the carapaces of 20,000 crabs. The machine will do another 20,000, for a total of 500 to 550 bushels a day, at about eighty crabs to a bushel.

"Lump" and "Special" meat types go into separate one-pound plastic containers, which can be either sold fresh or pasteurized for longer shelf life. Legs and claws are tossed into a tub to be sent to a machine or tended to later by the pickers. What's left of the crab is conveyed by belt to a dumpster, eventually to be ground up and

Backyard with crab boxes on Smith Island

converted to chicken feed and fertilizer. The blue crab is a generous contributor to the life of the Bay.

Lee Wilson's father-in-law, Grant Lawson, nicknamed "Hon," has begun to phase off the water. He has been selling his pots and he's thinking of renting out his shanty at Jenkins Creek, on the outskirts of Crisfield. He is fifty years old and tired of being a waterman, tired of all the regulations, tired of the problems, tired of the wear and tear, happy that his wife has a secure job with the state. She works for the Department of Health and Mental Hygiene, taking samples of water from the shellfish beds and testing them. And he is happy that he himself has found another way to earn a living. Some years back, as a hobby, he began to frame marine and wildlife prints. He has now developed a business where he buys directly from artists, frames their work, then sells it to the public. He has a traveling gallery, visiting twenty to twenty-five wildlife shows a year to show his prints, which he frames in a little shop next to his house on Jenkins Creek. He's looking now for a permanent gallery. His brother once wrote a book about the Ward brothers, two Crisfielders renowned for their woodcarvings, and Hon, who understands the value of good public relations, made himself chief director of marketing for the book, promoting it during his circuit of wildlife shows. His friends also understand the value of good public relations, and they once elected Hon to the presidency of the Somerset County Waterman's Association. In that role, he was a determined lobbyist in Annapolis and a frequent letter writer to the newspapers around the Bay. He says such things as, "The Department of Natural Resources doesn't want to take on a project unless they can really screw it up."

Lawsons reputedly have been saying things like that since 1609, when the first Lawson arrived in this country. Sailmakers and shipbuilders they were, and in time they migrated up the Bay, some going west and eventually to Tennessee and Kentucky, others coming up the Eastern Shore to Maryland. Lawson followed his father onto the water, although he took time off to serve with the U.S. Marines in Korea and to work at Sparrows Point, for Bethlehem Steel. He returned to Crisfield in 1969 and purchased a laundromat. But he quickly tired of emptying washers that wouldn't spin because they had been stuffed with blankets and quilts. He sold out and went back on the water.

The 1974–75 season was his best in crabs—he made $37,000 that summer. "You can still have a $30,000 summer, but everything costs more," said Lawson one evening outside his fishing shack on Jenkins Creek, a tiny harbor that may be the prettiest composition of marsh, sky, and boats on the Lower Eastern Shore. Lawson was "fishing up,"

Checking shedding trays, Smith Island

taking the soft crabs out of their shedding trays. Lawson would fish up again around 8 or 9 p.m. and be back by 4 a.m. Peelers were getting $12 a dozen. ''I'm almost married to it,'' he said. ''I have had a $14,000 week. If I'm lucky I like to shoot for $1,000 a week for the summer, about twenty weeks.''

Lawson's father carried him while he was getting started. Then, when his father got older and no longer could operate his boat, his son carried him. ''About the time he gave up,'' said Lawson, ''the industry went to hell.'' He cited a litany of problems that represent the industry going to hell:

Expenses. ''Crabpots used to cost $5; now, they're $11. Gas, thirty-two cents; now, $1. Boat expenses average $125 a week, $60 for electricity to keep the fish tanks circulating, $60 a day for bait, $200 for crew, $100 a week in wear and tear on your pots; it adds up to between $500 and $700 a week in expenses. You've got $60,000 in a boat by the time it's rigged up.''

Waterman Kie Tyler, Jenkins Creek

Thievery. "People steal. They'll pull five or six pots before they will pay $12 for my crabs."

Increased competition. "Venezuela puts crabmeat on the market cheaper than we can. The southern crab and oyster hurt us. They're producing oysters twelve months a year in Louisiana. We're only producing six months."

Physical problems. Lawson is a big man with a broad chest in an occupation where a man needs good legs, but a big waterman needs especially strong legs. His knees began to go to hell from lifting and pulling sixty- to seventy-pound pots full of crabs and nettles. "No way you can lift it right," he said. "You gotta reach over. You do it with your back, do it 300 to 500 times a day." He worked two years with torn muscles and cartilage in his knees. By the end of a day on the water, his legs would be so swollen he could barely get his pants off. He finally had both of his knees rebuilt.

Lawson has had a running battle with the DNR. "Christ, we need the DNR," he said. "The average waterman only sees what's in his boat. But the way DNR is now, they're no damned good. We need someone who can control the Bay. DNR is a big bureaucracy. Their main

Soft-shell crabber off Smith Island

job is conservation of the resource, but they want total control of the seafood industry. That's not their job. There's pressure from DNR for all sorts of restrictions: to make the crab floats bigger; to use cotton ropes instead of nylon. You can't use a two-gallon buoy on a crab. The wind would blow it off. Cotton ropes wear out two or three times a year. We can't set a pot in any river, in any of the marked channels, only in the Bay and the Sound. If boats can't stay in the channels between buoys, it's their own damned fault if the pot wraps a propeller.

"DNR wants to lease out (restrict) the bottom of the Bay to the oyster industry, the conglomerates. The Bay is my heritage; that belongs to me out there. My daddy couldn't leave me with a farm or a business. He left me knowledge, and the ability to follow the Bay. DNR has no right to take it away from me.

"Today, we're probably fishing one-third of the bottom we used to fish ten years ago. Probably producing the same number of oysters, which means we're really raking the bottom. Pollution is the reason for the decline in oysters. I'd like to see the Bay cleaned up, but you don't fight fire by shooting an extinguisher at the top. You go to the base. The solution is to clean up industry.

"I have no objection to the conservation of fish. I can't see the recent state ban on catching rockfish bringing it back; but I can't see catching the last rockfish myself either. Commercial fishermen won't catch the last fish in the Bay, as all the sportfishermen claim; no, sportfishermen will. Commercial watermen will switch to another industry if we can't make a living at it.

"The recent Critical Areas Bill, which prohibits development within a thousand feet of the shoreline on Maryland's coastal waters, is way too late, too weak. I say this as a waterman—less development will mean fewer people, less pollution. But, as a resident of Somerset County, the bill will destroy us. A lot of people, all they have is property. Now the Critical Areas Bill says you need twenty acres for a homesite. What do I do with this property? What value does it have? Why pay taxes on it? I can't use it. I should give it to the county.

"We need industry, but the environmentalists have killed off industry. The seafood industry is dying. This Bay is not getting better; it's getting worse. I don't know what the answer is. Tourists come through Crisfield, but they don't stop. We don't have anything. I am caught in the middle, confused. The little man is hurt first. I'm like the farmer—all he knows is he can't pay his bills and doesn't know who to blame. Someone's repossessing the Bay, and I don't know who it is."

Tim Carson left the water in 1978. That was the year his father died, and he had to decide in five minutes whether to stay on the water with no retirement benefits or take over managing The Pines Motel in Crisfield and earn a more secure living. He opted for the more secure

Overleaf: *Conch dredger off Cape Charles*

living. He lives two minutes away from the site of the Tawes crab feast, but even if he could afford the time, he wouldn't be caught dead paying $18.50 to stand in the sun and watch a bunch of people eat crabs and get blasted.

One evening, he drove his pickup truck to get some cold beer. When he returned, he parked it so he could see all twenty-eight rooms at his motel and was visible if any of the guests wanted him. His house was behind him, and somewhere inside it were his wife, Pat—a native Crisfielder, as he is, who teaches science at the high school—and their two small children. Carson sat inside the truck with a beer in his hand. He was wearing his standard motel manager's uniform, a white T-shirt and blue jeans. He is tall, with straight blond hair, blue eyes, and a nose that's on fire all summer long from the sun. Mosquitoes swarmed all around, but he did not notice them. To Carson, it is a beautiful summer evening when there is full occupancy, no one after him for anything, and a nice, round sun setting over Room 26. It was a beautiful evening.

"I miss turning that key in the boat," said Carson. "I worked the Pocomoke Sound, through Broad Creek. When I left the harbor to go to Broad Creek, no matter what the problem, I forgot about it. It was left behind. If you had never realized God or Nature was the Supreme Being, you realized it going through Broad Creek. Broad Creek was the unwinding point, the instrument that happened to be there. It was a natural high for me, like a man in a bar drinking to forget.

"Here in the motel business, there's no natural high. It's not the same. I like the people I work with, but it is not the same. I still answer phones all night long; some of the people get on my nerves; I can't hide; I can't go to the bar. There wasn't a lot I didn't like about the water.

Virginia waterman

Net fishing for menhaden near Norfolk, Virginia

I didn't like the sea nettles or the cold, but I could say, 'The hell with it,' and come home. Here, I am not my own boss. Everybody in the motel is my boss. I have to satisfy all twenty-eight rooms from beginning to end. If I lose my cool here, it affects the whole business. Out on the water, if I lost my cool, it would affect one or two days."

Carson worked on the water from 1973 to 1978, six years. He oystered, crabbed, and fished commercially for rockfish behind Tangier and Smith islands, using drift nets that moved with the tide. "It was like pulling a one-armed bandit—the thrill of never knowing what you were going to catch. Crabbing is boring—there's no unknown."

When he was a commercial fisherman, he would leave at 4 a.m. and return after dark. Sometimes he'd go thirty days straight that way, catching a ton or more of fish a day, never seeing Crisfield in the light, going out on days when he didn't belong out there because of the weather. "I've gotten home at nights," said Carson, "where I lay in the tub, talked to my wife ten or fifteen minutes, ate, and slept. That was the extent of family life during fishing season, day-in and day-out." His wife used to do the fishing up of the peelers when he was on the water. Their shanty at Jenkins Creek, built out over the water on stilts, was fixed up with a bed that his wife used during peeler time. She'd arise at 3:30, put the Beatles or Beach Boys on her four-speaker stereo— loud enough so she could hear it outside—and tend her crabs.

Carson had pinned the change from the six-pack of beer to the visor of his truck. His boss from Room 6 came striding toward the truck, looking for bug spray. The phone rang in the office, and Carson got out of the truck to check in his arriving boss in Room 14. "I've been away one night in eight years," he said when he returned. "That can last until I go crazy." His boss in Room 19 spotted Carson and came over to find out the identity of a certain flower, which Carson did not know.

"How the hell am I going to sleep tonight not knowing that flower?" asked his Room 19 boss.

"Would you like a beer instead?" asked Carson.

"You expect a good night's sleep, and the manager doesn't even know the name of a flower."

His boss from Pittsburgh in Room 16 comes for twelve days each summer to fish. Carson has lots of return business, bosses from New Jersey, Pennsylvania, New York, lots of repeat business because The Pines is clean, friendly, and has hot coffee and doughnuts in the lobby every morning when the doughnut truck gets there from Salisbury. Crisfield does not have a bakery. The Pines is also a place where Carson or his wife might jump in the truck with a plate of sweet potato biscuits and give a Crisfield newcomer a cook's tour. "I have to sell 'em the whole nine yards—a good meal, good room, tell them exactly what they want. I can't wait for them to ask questions. I tell them at the start what the town offers.

"If I hired a manager," said Carson, "and he abused the people in Room 16, it would eat my heart out. Rooms 21 and 22 brought me peaches from western Maryland. Room 15 is a retired lawyer from Syracuse, New York; been coming here for five years. The guy in Room 21 has been coming for eighteen years; the guy in Room 19 is from Florida, coming for five or six years. I have a man from Baltimore, a retired exterminator, comes every year. I'm a psychiatrist—people come here and like to talk."

At forty-two, Carson doesn't require a lot of sleep, maybe five or six hours, and is known to get up at three in the morning and walk around the grounds of the motel. His dad owned an auto parts business, a movie theater, a restaurant, and the motel. Carson went off to a two-year business college in Delaware before he transferred to the University of Baltimore and took a degree in marketing and accounting. Vietnam got eleven months of his time, as a Coast Guardsman assigned to board and search junks suspected of carrying supplies to the enemy.

In 1978, the year Carson had to make his five-minute decision, The Pines was the only motel in town, and it had thirteen units that never filled up. Today there are two motels, and both are filled many nights of the year. The tourist business has grown, thanks to fishing and to Tangier and Smith islands, the main attractions.

"Rooms 17 and 18 are going to Tangier tomorrow," said Carson, "21 and 22 to Smith. Fourteen, 12, 11, and 10 went or are going. Twenty-nine is a man from California who bought a home on Smith. Two, 3, 4, 5 . . . seventeen rooms altogether went or are going to Smith or Tangier.

"Your middle-income families who can't afford Ocean City come to Crisfield. People say, 'If only Crisfield had a beach.' I'm glad Crisfield doesn't have a beach. A beach brings in young people with problems. I don't need full occupancy with young people. Give me the caliber of person that I have rather than full occupancy and trouble.

"In my heart, I think the Bay is going to get worse. When I was drift netting, I'd see big tankers blow out their bilges with raw sewage. The little boat owner dumps a can of oil and gets hung by the Coast Guard. When I was a boy, you could see a stump on the bottom ten feet below. Could almost see the rockfish bite before he bit the lure. Now you can't see your hand below the water."

Carson left the truck to grab the phone again, and then to give the swimming pool its last chlorine check of the day. "If fishing and crabbing stop, Tangier Sound becomes nonexistent," he said, straining in the fast-dimming light to check the chlorine level in the only body of water he would see that day. He sold his boat five years ago because he didn't have time for it. "When the Bay dies, this area dies and everybody with it, because they're completely dependent on the water. They'll work the water until the day they die.

"The stability of a motel is better than the stability of life on the water. In all sincerity, I'd be a doggone fool to tell you money means nothing, but it's not the spearpoint of my life. Money is to buy those things in life we need as necessities, but it could never buy my experience going through Broad Creek. I'm one of those watermen caught in between."

The annual J. Millard Tawes Crab and Clam Bake is winding down. A half-hour before closing time at 4:30, the lines to the crab booth have disappeared; now the lines are in front of the portable toilets. The crab extravaganza is in the heavy-drinking phase of its agenda. The sun has turned crab orange. In the distance, the marina shimmers, a beery mirage. The masts and sails of boats form dark, slowly expanding, geometric patterns on the water. A soft breeze has come up to clear the air. Everywhere there are crab carcasses that will be swept into piles and taken away by trucks.

The next big crab event will be held on Labor Day weekend: the National Crab Derby signals the end of the crab season. In the meantime, there is work to be done on the Chesapeake Bay: crabs to catch, wilderness habitats to find and preserve, boats to repair or build, chickens and crops to raise, businesses to run, and problems, lots of

Overleaf: *Waterman off Tilghman Island*

Running a trot line for crabs

problems to solve. Complex problems that defy simple answers. Life-altering problems that are changing traditional ways of living on the Chesapeake Bay, and changing the character of the region. They are problems that require the combined efforts of all who need and love the Bay. Otherwise, for the hard-shell, hard-nosed, delectable crab, for all who need the Chesapeake Bay, the times, already tough, are going to get tougher.

Hunting
the Wilderness

The noise of the boat startles two blue-winged teal ahead on the creek. They squawk at the intrusion, and at the effort they have to make to get height above the marsh in the humid August air. A green heron, as still as driftwood, suddenly launches into flight. As the boat moves ahead, tiny silver fish pop out of the water on either side of the bow.

There are two men in the boat, one of whom is tall and slender with rosy cheeks, a large Adam's apple, and brown, curly hair as tangled as the grasses on the banks of the creek. Dressed in khaki pants and khaki shirt and standing in the bow, he has a pair of field binoculars around his neck. He scans the horizon periodically, but most of his attention is focused on the banks of the creek, which he studies with unusual scrutiny. The way he stands, he might be an explorer in some remote country, but instead of sturdy boots, he wears rubber "flip-flops."

"There is arrow arum, *Peltandra virginica,*" he says, in the clinical tone of a scientist making a routine observation. His Latin is smooth and unaffected, as natural as if he were calling a friend by name. He points to a plant in the water whose long, curved stalks end in large arrow-shaped leaves that are more than two feet long and brush the boat. Next to it is a plant with heart-shaped leaves and blue flowers. "*Pontederia cordata,* pickerelweed. Its flowers are real pretty, aren't they?" he asks. "There's some spatterdock, *Nuphar leuteum.*" He gestures toward a yellow pond-lily with leaves that float flat on the water at high tide but stand upright at low tide. Its flower resembles the yolk of a hard-boiled egg. "It's a good absorber of nutrients and pollutants that come into the marsh," he adds. "It's also a freshwater plant.

"There's seaside alder, *Alnus maritima,*" he continues, ticking off the flora. "It's believed Indians of the peninsula took its cones with them when they were moved to Oklahoma. Outside this area, Oklahoma is the only other state in which *Alnus maritima* is found. See the purple martin fly over the creek there? It dropped a fecal sack. The young defecate in their nest and the mother removes the feces so predators won't know by smell where the nest is. Look at the otter tracks on the bank. . . ." A pattern of indentations in the mud disappears quickly into a narrow tunnel of grasses whose stalks show the silt line, the discoloration caused by the tides. The water is a few inches below high tide. The creek is narrow, no more than five or six feet in places, a dark ribbon that winds back and forth through the marsh, which seems to stretch as far as the eye can see.

"We're in brackish water; there's lots of freshwater stuff here. This is a nice marsh, don't you think, Frank?" he asks his companion driving the boat.

"*Zizania aquatica,* wild rice, there to the left," says Frank, by way of response. He shuts off the motor and poles the boat toward a bank. The boat's forwardmost Latinist sits down and slips off his flip-flops in favor of some socks. He slides his feet into big rubber waders.

Natural erosion, Anne Arundel County

From his knapsack he retrieves a camera. He unfastens his belt and works it through a vasculum, the botanist's aluminum purse or handbag. Dressed for work, he steps out of the boat and sinks in up to his calf. The marsh sucks at his feet. He plunges on, searching out sedge mats to step onto, small clods of firmness in a sea of ooze. The sulfuric odor of marsh gas rises behind him.

"Ooooh, look at this," he says, bending down and pulling a hand lens from his vasculum. "It's a ten-petaled marsh pink, *Sabatia dodecandra*. Boy, I don't remember this much marsh pink—it's uncommon in Maryland." He takes a photograph, stooping almost to the level of the marsh to get a good close-up. When he's finished, he moves on, identifying one plant after another and calling out their Latin names while Frank, walking in another direction, calls back the Latin names of plants he sees.

The man's name is Daniel Boone, D. Daniel Boone. He is an explorer in search of rare plants and animals, and his frontier is a creek

that leads into the Nanticoke River on the Chesapeake Bay, a waterway surrounded by 14 million people. At the age of thirty, he is a botanist and ornithologist who spends his weekends hunting for rare habitats across the state of Maryland, and his working days as the coordinator of the Natural Heritage Program (NHP) for Maryland's Department of Natural Resources (DNR). NHP identifies endangered plants and animals and tries to protect them, or, as Boone puts it, "to lifeboat them into the future." "D" is for Darrell, his mother's idea to protect her son's future wife from a lifetime as Mrs. Daniel Boone. For the ten-thousandth time, he will say he likes his name and knows of no blood connection to his earlier namesake.

Frank's last name is Hirst. He is older by almost three decades and wears a cap that sits on his head like the pot of a plant turned upside-down. Running out from under it is a peeling red nose, a thin, white mustache, and a kindly smile. He lives in Stockton, east of Pocomoke, Maryland, where he owns thirty-three acres of soybeans and spends the majority of his time botanizing and fishing and teaching plumbing at a vocational school in Worcester County. "The big cordgrass there, *Spartina cynosuroides*," he says, "is a brackish water indicator. It's the largest of the *Spartina* genus, a cousin of *Spartina alterniflora*. It's a border grass and grows in either salt or fresh water."

The two men frequently botanize together on the Lower Eastern Shore, and Hirst occasionally does contract work for NHP. For this trip, they have traveled to a particular marsh on the Nanticoke River to inventory a special plant community, the fresh intertidal marsh, and to check on the well-being of a rare plant.

"It's the marsh wild senna, *Cassia fasciculata*, variety *macrosperma*," says Boone. Boone and Hirst sighted the plant in Maryland in 1984, the first time it had ever been seen in the state. It's on the Maryland endangered species list, and it's a candidate for the federal endangered species list. "This is the kind of habitat it lives in, a freshwater tidal marsh with a small feeder streamlet," says Boone. The marsh is freshwater tidal because when ocean tides come in the mouth of the Chesapeake Bay twice a day, and the flow of fresh water from the many rivers that drain into the Bay hits the elevated tidal level, the tide acts as a dam and backs up the fresh water into the upper reaches of the river.

Although the creek via which they have reached this marsh has a name and appears on the U.S. Geological Survey map for the quadrangle, Boone asks that it not be identified here. The marsh is one of the last remaining areas of wilderness in the region, and he wants it to remain that way as long as possible: "We live in a society where a lot of people are trophy hunters. They don't think it matters if you clip a rare plant to take home. We can't have it both ways, can't have a nice natural area and have everybody enjoying it. We can't love it to death.

Marshland, Lower Eastern Shore

I realize it's a contradiction, but some areas are extremely sensitive to human disturbances.''

The Nanticoke River, into which the creek flows, is perhaps the least well known of all the rivers of the Chesapeake Bay, and, happily for Boone, the least developed. Only thirty-six miles long, the river rises in Sussex County, Delaware, and is formed from the confluence of several creeks, the main ones being Gum Branch (which begins north near Staytonville, Delaware) and Deep Creek (which starts in the Redden State Forest, north of Georgetown, Delaware). The two creeks meet just east of Route 13, the major north-south artery for the Eastern Shore. Not far away is the biggest port on the river, Seaford, Delaware, importer of oil and chemicals, exporter of grain.

The Nanticoke enters Maryland above Sharptown. When it reaches Vienna, it begins to act like the Mississippi, meandering in sweeping curves and building up momentum to spread its waters all over creation. For most of its journey, the river is scarcely a quarter-mile wide, with a narrow main channel. It exits a tight S-turn at Long Point, about fifteen miles above its mouth, and immediately overruns its boundaries. By the time it joins Tangier Sound, the Nanticoke has become a sea of marsh, its mouth more than a mile wide, its shipping channel still a thin trench through a forest of sticks that appear to have fallen from the sky and stuck upright. They are put there by watermen to mark the edges of oyster beds.

Inside the mouth, on the eastern bank, there is firm ground where settlers founded the fishing villages of Bivalve, Tyaskin, and Nanticoke. The maladies associated with low ground, and the presence of Indians discouraged any significant further development of the river.

Nanticoke is the name of a branch of Delaware Indians whom Captain John Smith encountered during his exploration of the Chesapeake Bay in 1608. In his journal, Smith recorded that the Indians tried to entice his men to the shore. Suspecting ambush, Smith ordered a volley of gunfire aimed at them and at the thick grass cover along the edge of the marsh. The Indians fled, and when Smith went ashore, his crew found ''many blankets, and some blood, but saw not a savage.'' The Indians lived along the river in wigwam villages surrounded by stockades. Their main village was thought to be at the junction of the Nanticoke and its main tributary, the Marshyhope, a river-sized creek that splits off just below Sharptown and runs northwest through the town of Federalsburg. The Indians fished and trapped, built bark canoes, and were generally considered shrewd, though warlike, by the early colonists who traded with them. Eventually, the Nanticokes suffered the same fate as most American Indians and verged on extinction at the end of the eighteenth century, when Thomas Jefferson sent an emissary to document the Nanticoke language. Those who had not died had emigrated ''toward the frontiers,'' moving north to the banks of the Susquehanna in Pennsylvania, where they gave their name to a town just outside Wilkes-Barre, and farther north to Ontario, in Canada.

Otherwise, the history of the river is uneventful. Blackbeard the Pirate is supposed to have buried a treasure chest somewhere on the river, but no records exist that show he ever traveled up the Bay.

"Marshes are important," says Boone, referring to the most striking feature of the river and the entire Chesapeake Bay—its coastal marshlands. "Species live here that aren't found elsewhere in the state." Rich in grasses and plant life, the marshes are an essential link in the food chain. The mix of fresh and salt water creates what is by definition an estuary. Although more properly a river—the ancient drowned riverbed of the Susquehanna River, which today supplies more than half of the fresh water that enters the Bay—the Chesapeake Bay itself and all of its rivers are estuaries. Together, they form the largest estuary in the United States, and historically one of the most productive in the world. Its 64,000-square-mile watershed extends north from North Carolina almost to the border of Vermont. More than one-third of the country's population lives within that area, along with more than 2,700 species of animals and plants.

An estuary supports an especially large variety of plant and animal

Smith Island, Maryland

life. The grasses die and become food for bacteria and fungi, which in time are consumed by a variety of animals. The tides flush the detritus out of the marsh and provide food for the shell- and finfish found in coastal waters. Some sixty to eighty percent of fish valued commercially depend on estuaries for part or all of their life cycle. Bluefish and flounder make seasonal use of marshes for feeding, overwintering, or for nurseries. A major portion of the catch of oysters, clams, scallops, eels, alewives, and smelt is taken directly from salt marshes. Many kinds of wildfowl and mammals also rear young in marshes. In good years, up to 700,000 ducks may be raised in the southern coastal marshes. Many ducks, geese, and other waterfowl use marshes as resting and feeding stations during their migrations.

"Marshes are also a tremendous buffer for floods, and a filter for nutrients and toxins," says Boone, who, with Hirst, has mastered the art of marsh-walking and talking at the same time. Boone walks flat-footed with his knees bent. He looks like some strange khaki-clad heron as he probes with each foot before he commits to the next step. "If you destroy the marshes," he says, "fill them in, or drain them, you lose your buffer and the runoff goes into the Chesapeake Bay. When the habitat is destroyed, the species suffer.

"A poor maple tree having a tough fight." Boone points at a puny sapling whose roots are not genetically prepared for twice-daily tidal ablutions. A least bittern, orange in its upper body, blue on its bottom, flies into Boone's view. "That's a rare sight," he says, then adds, "A good sight.

"Six other species that live in an intertidal freshwater habitat like this are also endangered, close to extinction. The seaside alder is the most common one. It's endemic to the Bay, where there are thirty to fifty sites for it, but from a global perspective, it's pretty rare. Nuttall's hemianthus, *Micranthemum micranthemoides*, a wildflower that's off-cream in color and formerly grew in the fresh intertidal mudflats of the Bay and on several rivers of the Bay, hasn't been seen anywhere in the world since 1942. It may already be extinct. The sensitive joint-vetch, which still occurs in a few locales from North Carolina to New Jersey, now has only one known site in Maryland—in the Chesapeake area. I don't want to say where. It was once known in several places along the Patuxent River. Parker's pipewort is a federal candidate, as is the Maryland bur-marigold, *Bidens bidentoides*, variety *mariana*, Maryland's only truly endemic vascular plant. The *Bacopa stragula*, water hyssop, is in the same boat as the hemianthus—not seen in Maryland since the early 1940s, or late 1930s."

Boone stops suddenly and bends down. "Here's a *Lophotocarpus spongiosus*, or an arrowhead, as it's commonly known," he says with new excitement in his voice, indicating a plant low to the ground with thick, spongy, straplike leaves no more than five inches across. He

Anne Arundel County, Western Shore

touches the leaves gently, takes several photos, and makes some notes. It is the second recent sighting of the plant in Maryland. The first occurred two years ago at Vienna. Before that, the only documentation had taken place in the 1880s or 1890s, but Boone is not sure which.

"Nobody found it because they didn't have that German thing," says Hirst, smiling. He's referring to what Boone describes, somewhat mystically, as "marsh gestalt." "I have had a lot of experience," says Boone, taking Hirst dead seriously, "and the result is that a lot of little things pop into my mind. The range of microniches or microhabitats—each of hundreds of species has a little niche in the marsh, what I call a microniche—and the special geology, hydrology, and outside variables all play on a species and its requirements."

Changes in moisture gradient, for instance, because of hummocks and hillocks, seepage, tide, and a variety of hydrologic regimes, produce great diversity. Plants can perceive slight differences in water chemistry that humans cannot, and Boone has learned the distinguishing field characteristics.

"Half the skill in looking for plants is to put your mind in a state where you don't key on everything," says Boone. "It's very difficult to sustain an intense level of concentration—you'd end up looking at every individual plant. But your mind is prepared, you're keyed on the field marks that denote an unusual area." He is able to look at aerial and wetlands maps, and at color and infrared photos, and get a sense of where rare species occur based on secondary sources. "I've hit a lot of good areas. It's a combination of intuition, experience, and luck. You have to know what to look for. It takes years of field experience, and there's no rational explanation for how it works.

"It's that mental preparedness, and being able to utilize that knowledge in a way that defies rational analysis, that I describe as gestalt in the marsh. Another way to say it is that I'm programmed to know seven globally rare species could be found in this fresh intertidal habitat, let alone another twenty-five state-rare species."

Over the years, conservation groups have tried to preserve natural diversity generally in three ways. One was to seek to protect all unspoiled lands, although this often resulted in preserving mountaintops and doing nothing in the valleys. Two was to play a reactive role by responding to man-made threats of destruction to particular areas. Three, less predictable and less reliable, was to accept miscellaneous gifts of land from people who wanted to preserve their favorite places and gain a tax break at the same time. In recent years, The Nature Conservancy, a national private nonprofit organization founded in 1951, has adopted a fourth approach: locating and trying to preserve the biologically most critical and significant portions of the landscape, portions that, when taken together, contain the maximum amount of natural diversity. But to identify such areas requires "a systematic and comprehensive accumulation of ecological information."

Since 1974, The Conservancy has helped set up a Natural Heritage

DNR office, Annapolis

Program in more than forty states; Maryland's was established in 1979. NHP's two main functions are to make sure important habitats aren't destroyed through lack of knowledge, and to advise on protection efforts by the state, through acquisition, easements, and voluntary conservation and protection.

In 1984, Boone coauthored an article with Robert Chipley and George Fenwick in the publication *Threatened and Endangered Plants and Animals of Maryland,* in which they explained the program as, ". . . an ecological bookkeeping system with the database management system the ledger, and the elements of natural diversity the items on the ledger. Those already protected on preserved lands are in the assets column and those only existing on unprotected lands are in the debits column."

Boone's job in Maryland—where the Natural Heritage Program is a cooperative effort of The Nature Conservancy and the DNR—is to make sure that all elements of natural diversity in the state end up with at least some examples in the assets column.

The programs use basically the same methodology, testing all elements against two assumptions. First, if adequate examples of each habitat in Maryland were preserved—a salt marsh, for example—at least eighty-five percent of the species native to the state would be preserved. Second, preserving a representative cross section of habitats did not guarantee that species native to that habitat would be saved, because some species not only were rare, but were either not found in most

Overleaf: *Lower Eastern Shore*

habitats that seemed ideal for them or else were natives of very rare habitats. In this latter case, Boone's office drew up a list of endangered and rare plants and animals, incorporating the findings of all the state's experts. The elements were ranked in order of overall priority for research and protection efforts. Boone refers to it as the "Rarity Rank." It is divided into A's and B's. A's are nationally rare, most of them on, or candidates for, the federal endangered species list. B's are state-rare. There are about 600 A's and B's on the Rarity Rank at Boone's Annapolis headquarters, a modern glass-and-concrete four-story building next to the football stadium of the U.S. Naval Academy. "One result of our compiling a list," says Boone, "was the delisting of hundreds of elements found to be more common than originally supposed. Now we delist only a handful a year."

The key unit of information in the data management system is the "element occurrence": the occurrence of the element at a specific habitat locality that supports or otherwise contributes to the survival of one of those elements listed. For each element occurrence, a form is filled out and the information is computerized. The form includes information about the name of the element, the coordinates of its location, the date of observation or collection, the name of the source supplying that record, other sources that document that record, a site description, notes on the size of the population at that point, the name of the landowner, and an indication of whether or not this area is protected or preserved. Also included are general locators, such as name of county, physiographic province, and watershed. The computer provides the accessibility and flexibility to supply information in a variety of forms: all recorded localities for that species; all occurrences of all elements in a particular area; all the data supplied on element occurrences by a prominent botanist in the state.

NHP also keeps on file all 269 of the 7.5-minute U.S. Geological Survey topographic quadrangle maps for Maryland. "I love maps," says Boone. "They're just amazing. Maryland has outstanding maps, the finest in the country. Geological, topographical, road maps—we use them all to find rare species." The topographical maps are covered with multicolored dots to locate the exact occurrence of each element. Each dot is numbered and referenced to an entry in the margin that tells what that dot represents, be it the location of a rare plant, an endangered animal, or a community type. Yellow dots represent plants; green are natural communities such as a bog. Each dot has a whole sheet of data on the computer.

"Right now," says Boone, "we have about 5,000 element occurrence records for rare species and habitats in the computer. This allows us to retrieve and format the information instantaneously, and also allows us to store the records off the premises. It would take two to three years to replace the manually stored data if something like a fire ever happened."

NHP also has a computerized bibliography of information sources for rare species, habitats, and protected areas in the state, including names of experts and publications. NHP is also developing a database on species and their habitats, the biology and distribution of every species of vascular plant and vertebrate animal known for Maryland, nearly 4,000 species. It's called the Maryland Biological Inventory.

"We let the rare species dictate where important areas are," says Boone. "We're about as unbiased as can be. We don't go to an area and say, 'Oh, it's pretty. Let's protect it.' Methodology moves us away from bias. You record and study data, prioritize, bring objectivity to land preservation."

If the state wants to build a highway through an area, for instance, NHP looks at it and assesses the effects. If it affects a natural area, NHP will seek alternative alignments or recommend design modifications to avoid habitat destruction. The United States Soil Conservation Service (USSCS) is trying to channelize several hundred miles of streams and creeks in Maryland and Delaware that form the headwaters of the Upper Chester River. Channelizing means straightening out creeks—in effect, making ditches out of them to carry away runoff from fields. The ditches deliver farm fertilizer to the rivers and Bay, plus a huge pulse of fresh water that has been found to be acidic and to affect spawning. "One section of channel would affect a wetlands habitat for a very rare plant," Boone says. "I'm sensitive about revealing the name—there are only six known sites in the world." He visited the site about twenty times on his own and with various government officials before the USSCS finally decided not to proceed with its plan.

"It would be silly to preserve everything. You can't do it. That's where many environmentalists differ from me. They want to preserve it all; they equate all areas. They're not all the same, and the Natural Heritage Program tries to assign weights to different areas. By preserving a species, we don't mean we want to look it up in a museum. I want to preserve the last of the least and the best of the rest—that's a Nature Conservancy slogan. I want to see the best examples and the last examples of habitats we have in Maryland protected, so everybody in the future can enjoy them. I don't know what you call that, except at heart I'm a preservationist."

Boone used to spend three days at a time in the field, ranging over the entire state. Now, as the administrator for the program, he has to live vicariously through a staff of fifteen or twenty people. "I train them to develop a mental picture of the species and its habitat, a rare species image."

Boone's first rare species image was of a bird and not a plant. By the time he was thirteen or fourteen, he knew all the birds in Hagerstown, Maryland, where he grew up with a sister and an older brother named John, who taught Boone the shapes, sizes, and colors of different birds in Peterson's *Field Guide* until Dan, not yet able to read, could rattle them off by sight.

During his boyhood years, his bedroom window looked out on a cemetery full of dense growth. He would sit in a tree in the graveyard with a handful of suet until eventually the birds would eat from his hands. One night, lying awake in his bedroom, he heard an unfamiliar bird song coming from the cemetery, and he decided to find out what it was. He found the spot where the song had come from and began a watch that culminated in his sighting and identifying the willow flycatcher. It had never been found before in that part of Maryland.

The excitement of his discovery launched him into his career as a "passionate" ornithologist. He read all the bird books in the Washington County library and rode his bicycle all over town, finding birds that no one knew existed in Maryland, in such places as ponds behind drive-in theaters. He spent nights in the woods to learn more. He learned bird songs by tracking them down. "They fascinate me," he says. "Now I could probably identify 500 to 600 bird songs, including tropical ones, but that's no big deal—some people know thousands." By the time he was fifteen, he was leading birders from all over the state on trips around the county.

He and John decided to run a bluebird trail, putting up fifty bluebird boxes in some woods. In time, they built hundreds of boxes from lumber discarded at construction sites and nailed them up all over the area. They sought out farmers and educated them on the virtues of having nesting places for the birds. Long after his brother stopped, Dan ran three trails and, at one point, had more than 200 boxes. Checking the trails weekly took the entire weekend. The goal was to manage the boxes and raise the production of young. He kept detailed reports, recording the number of eggs and chasing away predators. Boone's trails produced several thousand birds. "The thrill was pulling off that many young," he recalls.

"I've probably seen close to 2,000 species of birds," says Boone, who has spent his vacations traveling all over the Americas looking for birds. "I don't know. I don't keep a life list. A lot of birdwatchers are what the British call 'tickers'—people who arrive at a site, see ten birds, tick them off their lists, and jump back in their cars. That's not real birdwatching. I want both to learn and to know.

"I marvel at the diversity of birds, the species, the plumage, the behavior. I couldn't in a lifetime grasp all the species—there are some 9,000 of them. I wonder how many of the 9,000 I could grasp if I were rich. If I were rich, I'd probably do something like that. I want to go to Australia because of the uniqueness of their birds, and to New Guinea to see the birds of paradise. I do like showy things; I'm not ashamed to admit it."

His birding interest exposed him to the wonders of wildflowers, grasses, trees, geological formations, and weather. An excellent student in high school, a fine basketball player, a good chess player, he received

Bird netting and tagging, Eastern Shore

a full scholarship to the University of Maryland, where he majored in biology and worked part-time at the Patuxent Wildlife Research Center. He graduated in 1978 and took a full-time job at the center, where his work schedule allowed him to develop a casual interest in plants into his life's work.

Exploring for bird habitats, he became interested in orchids. "There are some fifty species of orchids in Maryland alone—they are an amazingly diverse family," says Boone. "There are 25,000 species of orchids in the world, compared with only 650 breeding birds in North America. There are more vascular plants than vertebrate animals. There are nearly 3,000 species of vascular plants in Maryland alone.

"I went hunting one day for bog orchids. I'd been looking at bogs for days in a row and kept thinking, 'Damn, I find all these neat bogs, but no orchids.' Then, in a bog in western Maryland, in the space of ten minutes, I found two rare species: an Appalachian twayblade orchid last seen in Maryland in 1846, and an early coralroot, never found in the state before. I also found a creeping snowberry, a relative of the teaberry and the first recorded sighting in Maryland, and in the same bog, a hermit thrush's nest, also never before observed in Maryland.

"I was so excited, I wrote to The Nature Conservancy and said they ought to protect the bog. They wrote back, one thing led to another, and they offered me a job, which led eventually to the NHP."

Today, Boone lives outside Annapolis in an isolated farmhouse that is owned by DNR. The cluttered, frontier state of his quarters confirms that there is not yet a Mrs. D. Daniel Boone. He eats Mexican food from a nearby restaurant and is inclined to play his stereo loudly. Several of his splendid color photographs of wildflowers hang in the lobby at DNR, but to him, photography is only a means to an end. Like Martin Arrowsmith, Sinclair Lewis's fictitious hero who dedicated his life to science, Boone appears to have renounced the majority of earthly pleasures, such as money. He took a significant pay cut to become the coordinator of NHP. Most nights during the botanist's indoor season, he sits with his feet close to his wood-burning stove and thinks. "Thinking about plants and birds," he says, "is my favorite hobby next to looking for them."

The two marshland Latinists have slogged their way back to the boat and resumed their upstream journey. Cardinal flower, Virginia creeper, possum-haw—flora and fauna in this open-ended herbarium pass in review and Boone and Hirst rattle off their names, mixing Latin and English. It's part of their professional ego and their training to use the scientific Latin names. All field botanists do. That way, they avoid the confusion of the colloquial. Scientists in Mississippi

Overleaf: *Mill Creek, near Annapolis*

speak Latin so that scientists in Germany know what plants they are talking about. Boone studied three years of Latin in high school, but he learned the Latin names when he became serious about plants.

Hirst was three years out of high school and struggling with the Latin when he decided to confront it head-on. He took Gray's 2½-inch-thick botanist's manual for the Northeast and cut out the index of common names in order to force himself to learn the Latin ones. Hirst used to live in southern New Jersey, near a marsh, but every time he went fishing or hunting, he kept running into people, so he sold his plumbing business and moved to the Eastern Shore. In his new home state, he resumed his botanizing and soon developed a local renown for his knowledge of plants. One day in 1979, he received a call from a young man named Dan Boone, who had sighted a state-rare twayblade orchid in a bog and had been referred to Hirst as someone who knew quite a bit about plants. They liked each other and soon teamed up, traveling together as often as a dozen or more times a year in search of plants.

''Frank and I are a good team because we're both plant hounds,'' says Boone. ''We have the same drive to go on to an extra marsh to find something. It's the desire to find buried treasure. Frank has more experience. He taught me how to learn about grasses and sedges, rounded me out as a naturalist. I bring the focus of scientific urgency to conserve, the compelling urgency to find an area worthy of protection. Frank knows if we find a good area, there's a probability we can work within the system to protect it. That gives us an incentive. We're always trying to find an area before it gets destroyed. We know how to sift through an area that may seem nice, but may not be significant. We can sense a good area. We both have gestalt.''

Big, robust wild rice passes on the left. The ooze gives way to firmer marsh, and Boone and Hirst steer toward another bank. ''This is where we should see the marsh wild senna. It likes firmer ground,'' Boone says. The first time he and Hirst found it, they were actually looking for other fresh intertidal species like the sensitive joint-vetch. ''We didn't know what we had,'' recalls Boone, ''though we knew it was a *Cassia*. But, the marsh wild senna is a subspecies—now we're getting down to the nitty-gritty of taxonomy. It's one of a few plants whose species is not rare but whose subspecies is nationally rare. It's an anomaly—not a species, but a nationally significant variety. The NHP doesn't usually concern itself with varieties; we only concentrate on national and state-rare species unless the variety is nationally rare. We knew we had something different, but we weren't that excited because we had just found an arrowhead, which hadn't been seen in Maryland since the 1800s, and we were pretty high on that. We'd also found a rare mint, so the *Cassia* was just another thing. Last year, when we returned, we were mostly concerned with keeping tabs on the *Cassia*, hoping it was still there. It is one of the rarer plants we have, and it seems fairly stable.''

Boone and Hirst split up and move off to survey the marsh. In a short time, Boone calls out, "Here it is. See, it likes to grow near a little island of vegetation, which denotes firmer substrate." He fingers the plant gently. It grows about two feet high and has a diameter of about an inch. It is in full bloom, with bright yellow flowers. He leans close with his camera and takes several pictures. Then he resumes walking. He plods about fifty meters farther, turns at a right angle away from the creek, and negotiates an even greater distance before he returns to the marsh senna. "This patch is about 50 by 100 meters. It's not in here solidly, but it is well represented in the thicker vegetation, where the marsh is more firm. We've now found it on both sides of the creek, but the largest population is to the south. This patch is an example of a microniche, a special habitat." He and Hirst traipse around some more, then return to the boat, continuing inland.

Marshland soon turns to dry ground, trees, and undergrowth that crowds the shore. Some of the trees have fallen into the water and present obstacles around and under which the boat must maneuver. The creek has begun to twist and turn more sharply. Frank shuts off the motor and poles the boat around the many obstacles in the narrowing waterway. *Odocoileus virginianus* stands frozen in the shade—a white-tailed deer whose soft, summery brown is dappled where sunlight falls on its back. Deer are thought to be more plentiful here now than when the Indians lived along the shores. Farmers occasionally seek permits to hunt them out of season to prevent damage to their crops.

A silk blue dragonfly perches on a grass blade. Two blue herons, looking like small Hovercraft, get underway up ahead. "Frank, let's get the USSCS people in here to straighten out this creek. It's getting inconvenient for me to get to the wildlife." Boone laughs at his own suggestion. He stares at a thatch of grasses reaching out from a sunny bank. "I love grasses," he says. "I always like challenges, groups that others find difficult. Grasses are a bitch—infinitely more difficult than the supposedly confusing fall warblers. I think I like sedges more than grasses. There are 150 species of *Carex,* one of twelve genera of sedges in Maryland. I know most of those 150 species. They're keyed into so many different habitats. Most other botanists don't know the diversity of sedges; they concentrate more on wildflowers. I like the fact that they represent diversity. Grasses, sedges, and rushes make up more than twenty percent of our flora. Each family of plants has a nomenclature of its own. You have to start anew, with new terminology. For example, if you go from wildflowers to sedges, there are different terms for seeds, fruits, and stems. You have to learn how to key things out. Going from orchids to lilies is like going from reptiles to mammals. You can key out mammals using teeth, cranial structure. For plants, you have to know the diversity of terms.

"Goddamn, I gotta get that plant." Boone has leapt to his feet in the bow and appears ready to make an amphibious landing in the direction of a stand of grass growing to the left of a tree on the creek

Choptank River

bank. "I can't believe it!" Boone exclaims. "It's called *Chasmanthium latifolium,* wild oats, and it's the first time wild oats have been reported here in forty years." Hirst has brought the boat around to the bank where Boone has been steering him. He climbs out of the boat and onto the bank, but his hurry and excitement are transferred into a loving touch as he lays the tassel of the wild oats against his palm and studies it as if it were a long-lost work of art. He pulls out a plastic bag from his vasculum and clips a section of leaf and flower as a specimen. He will enter his find in the computer. "I had a feeling there were some wild plants up in here," says Boone settling back into the boat. Musing for a moment, he continues, "It sounds egotistical, but I'm at a different state of appreciation now. I get much more enjoyment out of appreciating an environment than I ever did out of a species. I can appreciate how plants and animals interact and interrelate. I cruise the woods and get a great thrill finding diversity. I really get off on learning about a habitat. That's where it's at.

"It's frustrating not to be able to get across to people that it's more than species; it's the habitat. You find a good habitat; it's protected by state law. Then some jerk wants to fill it in and he gets away with it. If you don't know what the habitats are, you can't conserve or protect very efficiently. We lost a rare species two years ago, a water beetle in a pond in Talbot County. We didn't really have enough information about it—didn't realize the significance of the habitat. The pond was bulldozed to make a duck habitat, and the beetle has never been seen again."

The distance between the silt line and the water has begun to widen noticeably. "Frank, I wouldn't want to be up here too long with the tide going out," says Boone. It is time to be poling out or the expedition may soon become a pole, walk, and carry affair. Hirst works the boat around on the narrow creek and poles back to deeper water, where he starts the motor. They retrace their journey through the creek back toward the Nanticoke.

"Look at that eat-out," says Hirst, as they once again enter open marshland. He points toward a brown circle as big as a softball infield. "*Ondatra zibethica,* muskrats. They like the tubers and leaves of plants, especially young plants whose roots are tender. Muskrats are disturbers of the marsh. So is fire. They are natural disturbers. Man is a disturber— he accelerates natural disturbances."

"Wetlands are a diminishing resource," says Boone, picking up on the thought of man as a disturber. "Tidal wetlands, like the salt marshes on the lower portions of this creek, have been protected for many years. But nontidal wetlands like we would find on the upper portion of this creek—swamps and bogs, which are much more diverse in the species they support—are less protected. We need to protect springs, swamps, and bogs—the perimeter around the uplands. When you clear a forest, you ruin the catchment for the spring; you alter the spring and change the hydrology of the watershed. What happens to the upland portion of our river system affects everything downstream. The ratio of nontidal to tidal wetlands is about three to one in Maryland. Nationally, we've lost millions and millions of acres of nontidal wetlands. Today, even with heightened efforts to save the Bay, the state of Virginia is losing 3,000 acres of wetlands per year; Maryland may be losing nearly that total as well."

"Malkus mallards," says Hirst at the sight of several ducks that, instead of taking flight, seem sure enough of themselves to remain on the water as the boat passes. "*Malkus mallards* is a derisive term used to describe dock sitters," he explains. "Ducks raised for hunters by the state, with money from hunting licenses. They lack the instinct to survive in the wild, to do much more than sit around on docks and defecate. They're also interbreeding with other species, such as the black duck, and breeding them out. They get their nickname from a state senator from Dorchester County who wants to make sure hunting doesn't die out as an industry in his region. The fact is, the state spends more money hatching and releasing these ducks than it would spend by buying them plucked, ready to cook, and handing them out to the hunters. The state should use the money to restore and preserve natural habitat for wild ducks.''

A bald eagle suddenly abandons its perch in a tree up ahead with a great flurry of activity, its white wing feathers shining in the sun. The status of the species has changed from 1895, when it was listed as common, to now, when it is listed as uncommon. The estimated breeding population in the Blackwater National Wildlife Refuge in Dorchester County on the western shore of the Nanticoke was about ten pairs in 1983. The bird is listed for Maryland as an endangered species by both the federal and state governments. ''To get on the endangered list, it helps to be an eagle, have big brown eyes, or be sexy,'' offers Boone, who then is hard pressed to name something on the endangered list that is ''sexy'' and withdraws that as a criterion. ''A disproportionate percentage of U.S. Fish and Wildlife research money gets spent on eagles. Fish and Wildlife tends to concentrate on high-profile or popular animals, to go after glamorous species. There are a tremendous number of systems unattended, systems that are not glamorous. The bald eagle is protected by federal law, but laws for protecting habitats are very limited.''

Boone has become aware of a new noise in the marsh—a distant whine to the southeast. He turns and shields his eyes. A tiny metallic dot shimmers in the sky above a line of trees. The noise expands to fill the marsh, and within seconds, *Homo sapiens technologicus*, a U.S. Navy jet, streaks overhead, low and ominous. Suddenly, it is gone, and with it, its terrible noise. ''I sure hope the Russians and the Americans get that defense system working,'' says Boone, laughing. Boone and Hirst are of another country, with different concerns about the environment.

Their approach to the river is heralded by the return of the greenhead fly, whose larvae grub about in the salty mud for snails and other invertebrate food, or eat each other. Every time the boat slows to negotiate a turn in the creek, handfuls of flies zoom in. Even Latin scholars are not immune to their bites. Hirst smacks one on his trousers and flicks it into the water. ''Trout food,'' he says.

In the summer, the Nanticoke Indians often moved their camp eastward to the windswept Atlantic shore to gain relief from the flies and their more numerous, hump-bodied comrades, the mosquitoes— of whom some seventy-five different species have been identified in the Chesapeake Bay region. They also smeared their bodies with fat rendered from bears or raccoons, or opossums, and lit smudge pots around their campfires. Early colonists adopted some of the same tactics, and watermen crabbing in the marshes during the summer have been known to cover themselves with oil and grease from their engines. Nor do wildlife escape the bloodthirsty tormenters that attack especially young birds and mammals unprotected by feathers and fur; the insects often kill them by exsanguination.

"More *Spartina*," observes Boone as the boat reaches the mouth of the creek. "The water is saltier here, about twelve to thirteen parts per 1,000 parts water. Salt is a great homogenizer. The more salt, the less diversity of plants and animals. Salt requires species adaptation to live. Thus, you lose competitiveness. Diversity is eliminated by the sheer requirement of living." Boone spies a yellow-billed cuckoo flying over the marsh. A turkey vulture soars in circles high overhead, riding the thermal currents. The silver minnows reappear on each side of the boat—infant menhaden, now the most heavily sought-after commercial fish in the Chesapeake. Menhaden are hunted with the aid of airplanes and netted in huge quantities to be crushed into fertilizer.

Creeks like this one on the upper reaches of the Nanticoke once were the most prolific spawning grounds on the Bay for another important commercial fish, the rockfish or striped bass. Watermen would lay hundreds of miles of gill nets across the rivers during the spawning runs. The apertures in a gill net are large enough to allow the fish to swim into them, but too small to allow fish under a certain size to pass all the way through. As the fish tries to back out, it becomes ensnared and usually drowns. Deadly efficient, the gill nets took a devastating toll. In the 1970s, scientists noticed an unusually high mortality among younger rockfish not accounted for by the gill-netting. Their studies suggested that an excess of toxins in the water—the by-products of ash emitted from coal-burning power plants, the dumpings of industry, pesticide and fertilizer runoff from farms—interfered with the normal growth of the fish's spine, resulting in a weakened skeleton that left the immature fish much more susceptible to danger and disease. Because of the dramatic decline in the fish harvest, the state banned all commercial and sportfishing for rockfish in 1986.

Emerging onto the Nanticoke River, Boone and Hirst see a hulking black barge being pushed upstream to Seaford by a tugboat whose superstructure towers above the marsh. An American flag on its stern points straight downriver. "Hey, that's boiling," says Frank. The bow of the barge is out of the water as the tug's twin screws churn up a wake that rolls toward each shore of the river. Two fishermen in a bassboat powered by a motor the size of a 747 jet engine speed into view on the far side of the barge. "Let 'em try and take that thing across the Bay," says Boone with a skepticism that reveals his low regard for expensive machines and contraptions that are not directly applicable to the science of botany.

In the distance, the smokestacks of the Delmarva Power and Light plant at Vienna come into view. Next to them are steel towers that carry

Power plant, Vienna, Maryland

power lines across the river. They rise above the flat landscape like twin Eiffel towers. Grass covers the opposite shore, as thick and impenetrable as a bamboo jungle, its top a sea of feathery tassels. "That's *Phragmites*," says Boone, a note of disillusionment in his voice. He does not like to see *Phragmites*. "It's known locally as 'the reed.' It likes disturbances, likes to grow where man has disturbed the environment. When they built the power plant, they filled in a lot of the marsh. That's where the *Phragmites* is. It gets in there and then takes over. It doesn't provide much food or cover for wildlife. Look, Frank, that section there—the *Phragmites* is dying off. Isn't that a shame?"

At a distance of a mile or more from Vienna, they notice a new noise. The drawbridge that crosses the Nanticoke at Vienna is steel grate, and every vehicle passing over it makes a whirring noise that travels up and down the river and into the marshes. A tourist who has sought out one of the town's new bed-and-breakfast establishments along the river hears the sound late at night, and awakens to it the next morning. If he should achieve the impossible and lose himself in the town's few streets, he can quickly reorient himself by listening for the bridge. On Fridays and Sundays during the summer, the noise becomes continuous as

Bridge at Vienna

thousands of cars and vans and trucks cross the bridge on the way to the Atlantic beaches at places such as Ocean City. The people come mostly from Washington, D.C., and Baltimore, and they follow Route 50, the main highway from the Western Shore to the Eastern Shore.

On each side of the drawbridge, a couple of miles distant, Route 50 narrows to two lanes to negotiate the bridge. The funnel backs up traffic for several miles. As the cars creep up to the Exxon station in Vienna, they stop for gas. The travelers want water. They want sodas. They want to use the bathroom. They want to vent their frustration with the heat and the traffic. But most of all, they want to get the hell out of this town with its monotonous view of river and marsh.

As the weekend traffic simmers and boils, the Nanticoke with its green bunting of marshland sweeps lazily under the bridge and off toward the Bay. Soon it will be fall and winter, and the marshes will change their colors and slow their rhythm of life. The traffic on Route 50 will dwindle to a trickle of birdwatchers and hunters—a predictable, seasonal change. But there are other more permanent changes at work

Overleaf: *Lower Eastern Shore*

in the marsh and throughout the Chesapeake Bay as man continues to accelerate the rate of disturbance. Wastewater from six states pours into the Bay, along with other detritus and sediment from eroding soil where land has been cleared and wetlands filled in. Vienna's town noise soon will become a thing of the past, because a new bridge is in the planning stages. Its span will be high enough to allow the passage of river traffic. Cars en route to and from the beaches no longer will have to slow down in Vienna. But easier transit will attract more people. "Come-downers," as the locals call people from outside the region, have already started buying property along the Nanticoke. The bridge will rise above marshland, and to accommodate the concrete pillars, the marsh will have to be filled in.

These changes notwithstanding, "the Nanticoke is one of the few Chesapeake rivers that still has a chance twenty or thirty years from now of looking like it does today," says Boone, eyeing the boat landing at Vienna where he and Hirst have left their cars and the boat trailer. "It all depends on what attitude we take toward development. If you feel man is the center of the universe, then there are no good arguments for protecting habitats and species. If you think man, plants, and animals are equal, there are lots of good arguments for preserving the species. But if you can't accept the argument of equality, then there's the argument about compassion. You should have compassion for future generations so they, too, can appreciate and derive benefits from our natural heritage. Our natural heritage is a legacy, and we should treat it as a legacy, not as a short-term gain."

The Endangered Craft

*A*t the turn of the last century, Sharptown, Maryland, on the southeast bank of the Nanticoke River, was an important supplier of two- to five-masted schooners to the Chesapeake region and beyond. In its glory years, the town boasted three garment factories, five grocery stores, two hotels, a skating rink, clothing and shoe stores, and a population of 900 to 1,000. The shipyards closed after World War I, and today all of the industry is gone, along with about one-third of the population. All that remains by way of industry is a pickle factory near the river, and that may not be around much longer if the town's citizens have their way. They have complained for years about the factory owner's seeming disregard for the unsightly appearance of his plant, and although it is unclear what they can do, they are increasingly determined to do something.

As a sign of the way things are in Sharptown today, the old steel trestle drawbridge is tired. The weight it can bear has been cut so that it can no longer accommodate loaded trucks. Since empty trucks arriving in Sharptown have no discernible economic value, the state is building a sleek, new, concrete bridge a block upriver.

The prospect of a new bridge helps confirm the bullish feeling that longtime Sharptown-watchers have about the town. They see the expanse of riverfront as central to its future as a retirement community and as a bedroom community for folks working in the DuPont nylon factory up in Seaford, or downriver in Vienna at Delmarva Power and Light. In short, Sharptown's biggest claim to fame right now is that it's a nice place to live.

One pillar of the old bridge abuts a ramshackle building with a faded sign that reads, LOWE'S SEAFOOD MARKET, an emporium regarded locally as the best around. It looks out toward the new bridge and toward a ballfield that lies approximately where the shipyards once were. Lowe's sign never changes its advertisements:

> RACCOONS
> MUSKRAT
> SHRIMP
> STEAMED CRABS
> FISH
> BLOODWORMS

Raccoons fetch $4.50 whole; muskrat, $1.50 whole, by the pair, frozen together inside plastic bags; grass shrimp from the Nanticoke, good for fishing, $3.50 a hundred; and steamed crabs at $7 a dozen after July 4, when crabs usually are more plentiful. You can also buy shad, herring roe, spot, flounder, and the *Cambridge Daily Banner*. The shad, Lowe is quick to point out, come from Delaware. Maryland prohibits the commercial fishing of shad.

It's neither here nor there, but Wick Lowe is a gourmet specialist in the arcane cuisine of raccoon and muskrat stew. He cooks two large dinners a year: one in Sharptown at the Legion Hall, where he prepares

thirty coons and 100 muskrats, and the other in Hebron, nine miles away, where the stew is fifteen coons and twenty-five muskrats larger than in Sharptown. He takes the stock from the boiled meat—which is dark like rabbit, with a musky flavor—mixes in Campbell's tomato soup, salt, pepper, sage, potatoes, and carrots; cooks it to a simmer; and serves it. Lowe is considered generous to a fault with the pepper.

Sixty years ago, had there been a coon feast in Sharptown, guests might have included passengers from steamboats that called regularly at towns along the Nanticoke, from after the Civil War until the early 1920s. They carried passengers and freight from Baltimore to Seaford, penetrating the farthest reaches of rivers and creeks to provide door-to-door delivery and pickup.

A visitor could board a steamer at Sharptown at noon, pay a one-way fare of $3.24, enjoy the highly polished brass and dark wood walls of the public rooms, eat dinner for seventy-five cents, supper for $1, spend the night in a stateroom that cost from $1.25 to $2.50, and eat breakfast for seventy-five cents, arriving shortly afterward in Baltimore. Dockworkers rang bells during foggy weather to guide the boats to the slips at stops such as Woodland, Truitt's, Sharptown, Riverton, Vienna, Lewis, Sandy Hill, Bivalve, Roaring Point, and Deal Island, before arriving at Baltimore.

The steamboats also carried farmers' produce, staples such as fertilizer and grain, and supplies needed for building ships: hardware, sails, rope, blocks, spikes, anchors, windlasses, cabin furniture, paint. There was no railroad through Sharptown, so farmers brought in their watermelons to be shipped to Baltimore, along with lumber and slab firewood from the mills. The Marvil Package Company of Sharptown, maker of baskets and crates for fruit and produce, imported gum logs from North Carolina, huge logs sometimes ten feet in diameter. The first copperhead snakes in Sharptown, and an occasional water moccasin, came courtesy of Marvil's gum logs. Eventually, shotgun-wielding crew stood watch over the barges in transit, and it got so that snakes couldn't stand the trip.

Because the Nanticoke had been one of the last rivers to be developed, it retained sizable tracts of virgin woods longer than other rivers whose banks and floodplains were deforested and converted to fields. Shipbuilders in Sharptown enjoyed access to an abundance of oak, white cedar, and pine. The banks of the river at Sharptown drop off naturally and do not require dredging, as they did at places like Vienna where the banks are flat. It was for these principal reasons that Sharptown and one particular upriver Delaware neighbor, Bethel, located on a tributary named Broad Creek, became shipbuilding centers.

Sharptown is small enough that when John Goslee drives his gray pickup from his house at the corner of 4th and Swan streets to the river across town, one of his dogs, a yellow Labrador, will chase along behind. Using a few shortcuts, as well as taking time to stop at Main Street in the unlikely event of traffic, the Lab can arrive within seconds of his master.

The town apparently is too big for Goslee's other dog, a cockapoo, a mixture of cocker spaniel and poodle that climbs into the truck cab, barks encouragement to the Lab, and generally raises cain.

Sharptown is not so small, however, that the Lab, on a quick turnaround trip, can match the truck going back. Neither the encouragement of the cockapoo nor the shortcuts help him keep up—he begins to tire and fall behind and finally stops to pee.

Goslee's Lab is just another Sharptown dog, but John Goslee is the sole survivor of Sharptown's shipbuilding industry.

John Goslee built his first boat, a sixteen-foot skiff, known as the Sharptown shad barge, when he was twelve, and as far as he knows, he is the only craftsman still building them. There are fifteen or twenty of his boats around the area, including one in the museum at St. Michaels.

Goslee is built like a compact pickup truck. He is solid, short, less than 5½ feet tall, and has one speed—all-out. He seldom sleeps more than three or four hours a night. He fuels his motor with food. He eats from the time he finishes dinner until he goes to bed, unless he has a boat in the works, in which case he may forget about dinner until breakfast time. He claims he could spend twenty-four hours a day in his workshop if it were not for his wife.

His fingers are the shape of fish sticks, rectangular and squared off at the ends. He wears glasses and builds almost anything anyone can imagine out of a piece of wood. Besides boats, he builds houses, chests, chairs, clocks, spinning wheels, oak kitchen tables, and bookends for a queen-sized bed. One week he'll build a doghouse, the next week a purple martin house in the shape of a miniature three-story Swiss chalet that is likely to set a new trend in architectural design for martin houses. He also repairs musical instruments and rehabilitates old machines, such as a 135-year-old family ice cream freezer that, by his estimate, has contributed some 5,000 gallons to the perpetual happiness of the Goslee family.

Sixty-one years old, he formerly worked as a yard manager for a big paper company, running a crane, but he hasn't worked since 1982. In the interim, he has been in the hospital twenty times for surgery on his heart, stomach, jaw, and feet. "My stomach is tore up," he says. "I had four operations in the same incision. I also broke my back in World War II, but I never let anything get me down, and I'm getting tougher every time."

On his three-quarter-acre property, in a workshop behind his house, is a Sharptown shad barge, a skiff originally designed by his great uncle. Measuring twenty-two feet long, it is built of four different woods:

John Goslee

yellow pine, white cedar, red cedar, and walnut. This particular boat is a showpiece, and it has been polished until it gleams.

"It took about six months to build this boat," says Goslee, "but I've built about 200 of them, some in as little as two weeks. They were designed right here in Sharptown many years ago to be used for fishing for shad. They carry as much as a ton of fish easy, a ton of anything. Its deepest draft is about 3½ or four inches—it depends on the length. It can float on a heavy dew, get right in on a mudflat. The bow and stern don't touch the water when the boat carries a light load. The heavier the load, the harder she goes down because of the flare in the sides."

Ranging from sixteen to twenty-four feet long, no two boats have the same measurements. That's because there are no plans— just guesswork. Their low washboards—twelve to fourteen inches high at midships—made it easy to pay out long drift nets. A man in the stern paddled, the man in the bow wrenched off with his paddle or pushed the blade away from the boat, forcing the boat sideways to avoid running over the net. Then they reversed; the bow man paddled, the stern man wrenched off. Front man threw out one cork of the net, stern man wrenched off. Working hand-in-glove, they could pay out 150 yards of net in about seven or eight minutes. Pulling the net in, the front man piled the corks in the bow; the stern man did the same, trapping the fish under the net. They usually carried at least two nets, often four.

"If the tide was running," says Goslee, "you'd let the net out from a reach in the river, from one turn to the next. One reach to the next may take ten to thirty minutes, depending on the strength of the tide." They fished both tides, fished all night long when they were catching them. If the wind blew from the south or west, there was bound to be good fishing. But a northeast or southeast wind was no good.

"I remember one day when we caught 360 pounds of roe shad on one tide with my dad. It wasn't anything to catch roe shad. Buck shad didn't bring more than two cents a pound; roe shad brought $1 apiece on the average. All that's gone by the wayside. You catch two shad a day now, if you're lucky. A lot of shad have come back, but the DNR claims they're scarce and won't let us catch any. It's like those rockfish. My land o' mercy, I never seen so many rock up here this summer. DNR says there weren't any."

"You can use shad boats and skiffs for pleasure, for hook/line fishing," says Goslee, switching to his role as salesman for the firm of Goslee, Inc. "It sets right up in the water like a duck." He runs his hand along the polished washboard. "This one's from an old-growth pine, almost 400 years old; it was crooked, but first rate as far as the lumber goes. I don't want a pine or oak out of low ground. Low-ground timber rots quicker. It grows faster because of the moisture. When trees grow

Overleaf: *Shad barges stored in boathouse on the Nanticoke River, Sharptown*

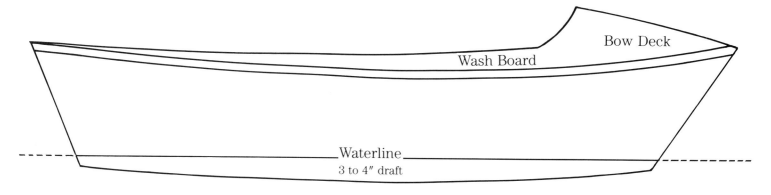

Wash Board

Bow Deck

Waterline
3 to 4″ draft

SIDE AND TOP VIEW

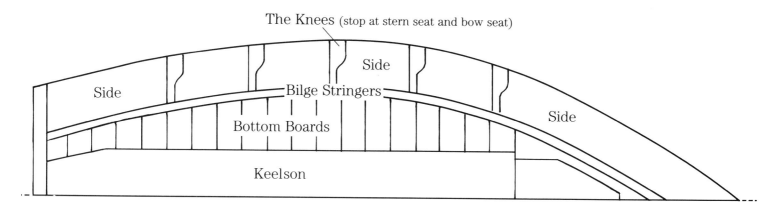

The Knees (stop at stern seat and bow seat)

Side

Side

Bilge Stringers

Bottom Boards

Side

Keelson

INSIDE HALF AND TOP VIEW

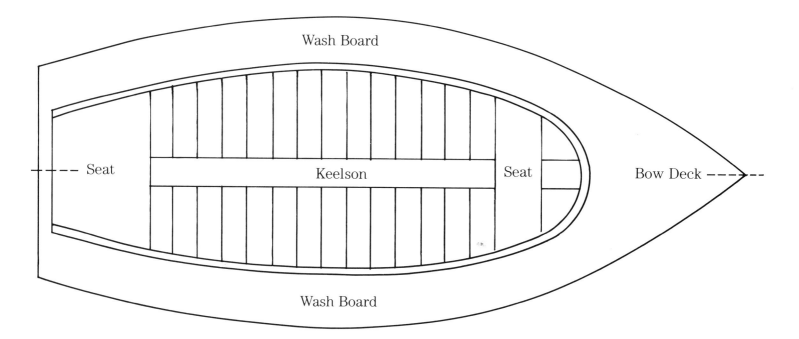

Wash Board

Seat

Keelson

Seat

Bow Deck

Wash Board

TOP VIEW

fast, they gets lots of summer wood, which is sappy, and that's what makes them rot. It takes cold winters and slow growth to make good timber. Slow growth makes a tighter grain. Summer wood is wider grained, softer. If I have a choice, I take a high-ground tree. The bottom of this boat is white cedar—it only grows on low land," he says, "but its pulp is more dense. The sides are foxtail pine, a virgin pine that was here when the Pilgrims came. The keelson [the boat's spine] is a solid piece of pine. I always use a thicker piece for strength and width—just as wide as I can get."

Goslee saws his planks of rough white cedar and pine on a sawmill once owned by his father. Now he and his brother own it. He first builds the stern out of a two-foot piece of black walnut—walnut doesn't swell or rot. "A stern that swells will split the sides of the boat," he says, "and then you got a job." A lot of people have told him he is crazy to put the expensive walnut in a boat stern. "Maybe ten years ago, you could get enough lumber from a local sawmill to build a boat for $60. Back when net fishing was in its heyday, twenty-five years ago, you could build one for $25. I don't worry about what it costs. I think about the job it's got to do. Good oak may be cheaper, but it's hard to find around here. It's small and buggy. I've used red cedar and mulberry in the stern, too. People never think of sawing up old mulberry or sassafras for a boat, but none of it causes trouble like oak. A lot of people call mulberry trashy wood, but it's real good. When it dries, it is just as tough and hard as it can be. I don't like mahogany on a boat; it's good for trim, but under the water, it gets wet and soft, comes apart, splinters."

Goslee shapes the sides—lays the sweep or flare—starting at the stem and working toward the stern. He braces the sides with a spreader stick fastened in the bow and another fastened in the middle, loops a rope around the stern, and twists it tight to bend the bow planks and bring them together. By working his way back, he produces the flare, thirty-four inches across the top at the stern, tapering to nineteen inches at the bottom. "The secret is knowing where and how much to take out, and how to set or open the flare so the boat lines look good. Then I add washboards that really brace the boat good and are like a table to lay your nets on."

Once he has the walnut knees in, Goslee fiberglasses the bottom and sides, clear up to the top edge of the washboards. Fiberglassing is durable, adds strength, is easy to clean, and doesn't leak. "By fiberglassing, I can leave the boat out in the sun for three months; otherwise, without fiberglass, the sun would dry it out."

He sells each boat for $1,000. It will take a twenty-foot mast and an engine up to thirty-five horsepower. "I'd go across the Bay in a minute in this, and I can't swim a stroke," says Goslee, returning to his role as salesman. "Two men can paddle it up to ten miles per hour when the tide and the wind are right."

A boater on the Nanticoke passing a shad barge piloted by Goslee is liable to hear the sound of an army bugle. During World War II, Goslee was a bugler, assigned to the last unit of horse cavalry at Fort Riley, Kansas, before he was transferred to the Third Army under General George Patton. On one occasion on the Nanticoke, he was stopped by the marine police and charged with not having a whistle. He blew his bugle and they let him go without a fine.

When Goslee's motor is idling, he sits in his comfortable house and drinks iced tea, as often as not from a mug that reads, "There's no life west of the Chesapeake Bay." If Goslee were emperor of the Eastern Shore, down would come the Bay Bridge. Ocean City would be walled in as if it were another Babylon and condemned to the ravages of the sea. The ills of the Delmarva Peninsula have been visited upon him and others like him by the DNR, by tourists, by upstaters who want to control the peninsula. "I can't hunt anymore," he says. "I can't afford to pay the farmers who rent their land to hunters from up north. You can't hardly get across Route 50 because of the traffic in the summer. There's a three-hour backup at Vienna bridge. The money is not staying on the Eastern Shore. It's become a rich man's playground. People have one thing in mind—Ocean City.

"Like I said, DNR has cut the rockfishing, even though there's more rock now than in the last ten years. Sportfishermen are behind the rock law. They want to drive out the commercial fishermen so they can have good sportfishing. Sportfishermen catch more than commercial fishermen, who only fish when the rock spawn or in the fall when the rock bunch up in the cooler water. In Virginia, you can still catch rock of any size. Anybody knows you can't expect a rock to spawn if it gets caught in Virginia and can't get here to spawn. The cleanup of the Bay needs to come from industry, from places like Sparrows Point [the Bethlehem Steel plant]. Not being able to build within 1,000 feet of the shoreline and requiring twenty acres for each home is hogwash," Goslee says, referring to the Critical Areas Bill. "I'll tell you the truth, it's all politics."

As for the future of the Sharptown shad barge industry: A reporter from the *Baltimore Sun* once did a story on Goslee, and in the months that followed, Goslee received orders for nine boats. The pace has slowed to one a year for several years now. The shad barge was in danger of becoming extinct, but it now appears that its natural life will be extended at least another generation. Goslee's oldest son, Jimmy, who is as handy as his father with metal and wood, has recently decided he wants his father to teach him how to build the boat.

Robert H. Burgess has written extensively about the Chesapeake Bay and may be the foremost authority on Chesapeake boats. In his book *Chesapeake Sailing Craft* (Tidewater Publishers, Cambridge, Maryland, 1975), he reports that the 1925 edition of *Merchant Vessels of the United*

Waterman throwing eel ashore from shad barge on the Nanticoke River

States listed "at least 720 sailing vessels registered out of the Chesapeake Bay ports of Baltimore, Annapolis, Crisfield, Cambridge, Washington, D.C., Alexandria, Reedville, Cape Charles, Newport News, and Norfolk, more commercial sailing craft than on any other body of water in the United States at that time.

"It was impossible," writes Burgess, "to make a trip on the Bay without seeing craft under sail or encountering them in the harbors of the largest ports or bayside towns." The number did not include the countless smaller sloops, schooners, pungies, bugeyes, rams, and skipjacks, most of which confined their activities to the Bay and its tributaries.

Sharptown and its upriver neighbors contributed, in particular, a wooden ship called the ram, an efficient sailing vessel that was shallow enough in draft for the Bay, narrow enough to pass through the locks of the Chesapeake and Delaware Canal, and seaworthy enough to make an Atlantic crossing. They sailed at a good speed, as much as ten knots in a fair breeze. A ram required only a small crew, no more than six to eight men, often fewer, and thus could offer an economy and efficiency that explains why James E. Marvil, M.D., in his book *Sailing Rams* (Sussex Press, Lewes, Delaware, 1974), describes the ram as "one of the toughest and most profitable three-masted schooners of all time."

The ram usually was built for a specific captain, who would sell shares in the boat to raise money to underwrite the construction costs. The prospects of a twelve-to-twenty-percent return on their investment made shares in ships fairly easy to sell. Ship brokers and chandlers frequently purchased shares and in return received orders for sails and other items needed for the ships.

Oak from nearby swamps—such as the one at Gumboro, Delaware— was popular, especially when it was green and could be worked easily. Oak was preferred because it shrinks considerably and would hold the fastenings more tightly. The ram's keel was of oak timber, ten inches by twelve inches, as long as possible. The bow portion of the keel rose to five feet off the ground and tapered at the stern to about two or three feet. After the keel was laid, eight-by-ten-inch oak cross timbers were put in place for flooring, eighteen inches on center, and left unbolted. The building then proceeded apace, with the initial work crew of fifteen to twenty-five carpenters increasing to fifty or sixty men working on one boat. The work was both a community and an intergenerational effort. John Goslee's grandfather and uncle on his mother's side ran the sail loft or made the sails in the shipyard at Sharptown.

On launching day in Sharptown, the schools and most of the town shut down. Ships were often launched on Fridays so the town could celebrate until Sunday. The launchings caused such excitement that on at least two different occasions, fires that broke out in town went unnoticed until it was almost too late to prevent a major conflagration.

Skipjacks moored at Tilghman Island

The actual moment of launching occurred when the flood tide had just begun to ebb. The ship would slide down the skids and hit the water with a huge splash, sending an enormous wave up and down the river. The ship would travel for several hundred yards upriver, but it would start to return on the ebbing tide. Then the workmen would secure the ship to the dock and finish it off.

The men who mastered Chesapeake-built sailing ships traveled the world but chose—many of them—to return home to the Eastern Shore, to places such as Bethel. The tiny little village of white cottages and houses with picket fences seems to have been picked up, lock, stock, and barrel, from some corner of the New England Coast and set down beneath the huge shady trees on the banks of Broad Creek. Today, it is an anomaly in the maritime history of the Chesapeake, a quiet backwater surrounded by fields of melon and corn. There is an old Bethel saying attributed to the women of the town: ''I don't want to marry a farmer that scratches in the dirt, I want to marry a sailor who wears a ruffled shirt.'' It stems from a time when jobs in Bethel meant going to sea. Every house in town seems to have sent its men to the ships at one time or another, especially at the turn of the last century.

''In the 1920s and 30s, age began to take its toll markedly among the Chesapeake's sailing vessels,'' writes Burgess. ''Most of the schooners still in service at that time had been built in the 1840s and 50s. Many had, no doubt, been rebuilt but had eventually become or were becoming waterlogged, structurally unsound, too expensive to continue to repair, especially as the volume of freight fell off in favor of motorized land transport.'' Although the extensive waterways of the Chesapeake made it feasible to continue operating sailing vessels long after they had disappeared from other American ports, when the *Jennie D. Bell* lowered her sails for the last time in 1954, only the Maryland oyster dredgers were left to uphold the tradition of sail on the Chesapeake. How long they would last, said Burgess, depended on the uncertain future of the oyster industry.

As sails were replaced by engines, the masters of sail moved on, too, but not without regret. Captain Vernon T. Hopkins talked wistfully about life before the mast of a ram in an interview that Dr. Marvil cites from the August 4, 1968, edition of the *Salisbury Sunday Times*, when Hopkins then was ninety years old.

> Sailing's long gone, well gone. We never had enough men,
> with only four sailors, a cook and the master to handle a
> vessel. We'd be wet and cold, soaked through for days on
> end in bad weather; knocked about, sore; just beat from the
> long hours on deck. But then, when the sun did come out
> and we got a long run with favoring winds, that was all

Cemetery at Sharptown

forgot. This was living. Sails set, an easy wheel—there
has never been anything like it. It was a pretty thing.

"Burn the wooden sons of bitches" is the prevailing attitude
toward traditional Chesapeake workboats at Evans Boat Repair on
7th Street in Crisfield, Maryland. Eugene Evans will repair wooden
boats, but he would rather build a fiberglass boat, and he's staked
his livelihood on nonwooden, nontraditional workboats. So have
an increasing number of other watermen.

A native of Smith Island, Evans, age thirty-four, did what his father
and his father-in-law had done—went to work on the water. But "the
water business is a hard life," he says. He developed acute tendonitis
in both arms from constantly lifting loaded crabpots. The physical rigor,
the insecurity of such a life, and the unproductive dead time when he
had to "lay-in" in bad weather or between fishing seasons, began to get
to him. So did the endless task of having to maintain his wooden boat.
He owned three wooden boats in succession—loved them like a family
with three Chevrolets.

Three years ago, in the face of what he thought were increasingly
grim prospects for his future as a fisherman, he switched careers and
began repairing wooden boats. Along the way he was converted to
fiberglass boats, an experience that appears to have been quasi-religious,
judging by the fervor with which he now embraces the future.

"Fiberglass boats are stronger, lighter, more buoyant," he says as
he stands in the resin-rich air of his workshop. Evans and his workmen
have fiberglassed their respiratory and olfactory systems to such an
extent that they do not seem to notice the thick, headaching odors of the
polyester resins that are mixed with hardeners to cover the fiberglass.
"Wooden boats," he says, pausing as if he were trying to recall an
artifact that he had seen once as a small child, "are always having to
be repaired; you have to railway the boat twice a year, between seasons.
It used to be you could do it between crab and oyster season. Now, you
can't afford to take two weeks off to attend the boat between seasons.
You need the money and you have to have the boat on the water to
earn the money.

"I got tired of wood boats: scraping, sanding; having to renail,
caulk, paint. I wanted a fiberglass boat tough enough to break through
a half-inch or more of ice going to Smith Island. Thin ice is hard on a
wood boat. It's like window pane. Cuts it up bad. And there's fuel
maintenance. My dad had an old wooden boat and it used to take him
1¼ hours to get to the crab grounds. Now he can do it in twenty-five
minutes. A thirty-foot fiberglass boat with a four-cylinder engine can go
twenty-five to thirty miles per hour comfortably and save fifty percent
on gas. You can pay her bank notes on the gas saved.

"They're good for crab scraping. You don't have to worry about

Fiberglass hull, Church Creek, Maryland

Building mold for fiberglass hull, Fishing Creek, Maryland

fiberglass boats laying in the wind. When it's blowing twenty miles an hour and you're in fourteen inches of water dragging crab scrapes and having to turn on the quarter, with a glass boat you don't have to worry about blowing over the top of the other scrape. Fiberglass will outhandle any wooden boat at least thirty percent better. They won't let fiberglass boats race in the same class as wooden boats.''

Evans can complete a thirty-foot boat in three weeks. He begins by building a wooden frame, or mold, using plywood cutouts as if he were sewing dresses by laying down Singer patterns on the material. He builds the molds himself, something of an art. His wife, Rose, a Smith Islander who serves as secretary, office manager, and public relations manager for her husband, says there isn't anything the dark-haired ex-waterman can't build or fix. He can mold boats ranging from fifteen to forty feet long. Sheets of fiberglass are attached to the wood molds and covered with a mixture of thirty-five cubic centimeters of hardener to one gallon of resin. When the glass hardens, the sides of the mold are pried apart, then flushed with water until the entire boat pops free. Evans then flips the boat over and puts on the skeg or keel. Once the keel is attached, he sands the boat and paints it.

Evans does about five things at a time, and what he doesn't get done, Rose is doing in the office inside. He began his business with three helpers; he now has fifteen and two businesses. The second one is a marine hardware dealership, which includes Volvo engines. When his workshop began bursting at the seams with boats in various stages of construction and repair, Evans finally decided to build a larger facility, which he did alongside Route 413 farther uptown. He sold twenty-five

Preparing for annual resurfacing, Taylor Island

boats last year, at upward of $16,000 each, including an engine that he provides courtesy of his Volvo distributorship. ''They're a lot less expensive after the initial buy,'' says Evans. ''The biggest problem is that people can't afford the initial cost. They're satisfied with what they got, but it's the Chevrolet-versus-Cadillac argument—deep down in your heart, you'd like to have a Cadillac, but you get what you can afford.''

A lot of former Chevy owners seem able to afford Evans's prices, which he claims are ten percent lower than most dealers'. He has a six-month backlog of orders and his customers come from all over. He recently sold a boat to a man living in Ohio who took it to the Florida Keys. A couple from Tennessee came to see his boats this past spring. He advertises in the *National Fisherman* and travels on weekends to boat shows and marinas up and down the Bay. During warm weather, he combines business and pleasure by visiting around the Bay aboard his own fiberglass boat. Now that he doesn't have to work on the water six days a week, he enjoys being on the water with his two children. He's building a larger, forty-two-foot fiberglass boat fitted out with bunks and enough hardware to catch any mariner's eye. He intends to drive it all over the Bay for advertising.

''When I was twenty, my goal was to be able to take it easier at forty than I seen watermen taking it at sixty. I seen a sixty-two-year-old waterman work harder than someone half his age. That's their whole life. I didn't want that. I want to live to be able to retire comfortable. I want to build a business and be the best I can. Being rich is not my goal.''

As for the dark side of boatbuilding—the possibility that commercial fishing might die out in the Chesapeake—he doesn't think much about it. ''It's always been commercial fishermen. I think I was reading somewhere that we eat almost as much seafood each day as we do farm food in this country. As for the wooden boats themselves, they don't let wood season the way it should anymore,'' he says, preparing to resume his full load of tasks. ''Today, if you go five years without bad wood, you're lucky. Five years is the natural life of a wooden boat.

''I give wooden boat customers the same deals. I can't help it if a man likes a wood boat versus a fiberglass one. But the traditional attitude where a waterman would say he wanted a wooden boat 'cause that's what his father had, that's what he's used to, that's changing. In the next ten or fifteen years, you'll see lots of people changing and updating their rigs. I am not naive enough to say wooden boats are soon going to be depleted. I don't think you'll ever see there's no wooden boats. It's like saying all the old cars on the road will be gone. No, they'll still be around; people will still be driving old cars. It's the same with wooden boats.''

''I'm not interested in boats, never owned one, not interested in the water, and don't like to fish,'' says George Raye. His words come

Rye field, Sharptown

close to heresy in a region where everyone seems to have some connection to the water. Raye doesn't even live near the water. He raises roaster chickens for the Perdue Corporation on a 119-acre farm located inland on the Delaware-Maryland state line near Salisbury.

The farm itself presents nothing extraordinary to the passerby. It has the customary Eastern Shore look: white house, barn, and two low, block-long chicken houses that accommodate 32,000 growing chickens. In his side yard, half a dozen or more weathered gravestones lean at different angles above the freshly mowed grass. Raye's family had this farm long before there were Perdue chickens, even before there were railroads. They have lived here more than 200 years, and some of them—although Raye is not certain which ones—are buried in his yard. Beyond the expansive, well-kept yard, fields of soybeans stretch almost to the horizon, right up to a dark line of trees. No traffic ever seems to travel the narrow county road. The farm seems quiet and calm. Often, the only signs of life are a pair of workboots by the screened-porch door and Raye's dog rising slowly from the grass to limp forward in docile greeting.

While the Perdue agent who regularly checks Raye's brood may consider him to be just another chicken farmer, he is different from the rest of the ever-growing flock of chicken farmers on the Eastern Shore. What makes him different is what he does in the big, white barn behind his house.

On a late summer afternoon, Raye stands in the doorway of his barn, one foot on a pitchfork, his hazel eyes moving on and off eye contact with his visitor. He wears ankle-high construction boots, heavy tan pants, and a workshirt with a mechanical pencil in his pocket. At age forty-three, blond, with a mustache and a shy smile, he is built as solidly as the keelson on a workboat.

He pulls out the pitchfork and leans it against the side of the barn. The tiny hairs on his arms are gold flecks in the sun, which slants through the open door into the barn. A fine dust diffuses the light and gives the high-ceilinged interior the muted light of a cathedral. The inside is cool and peaceful. The floor is carpeted thickly in sawdust and shavings, and tools and odd pieces of lumber are strewn about. Only the center of the barn remains clear and open.

In the center of the center, conceived on dry land, miles from open water, stands the half-finished skeleton of a boat that runs almost the length of the barn. It is the beginning of a Chesapeake deadrise workboat. Raye, the chicken-farming nonwaterman, builds workboats in his barn for watermen. He has built seventeen of these craft, which range from thirty-eight to forty-two feet in length. Their telltale mark is a vee-bottomed bow that rises above the full height of a man, then tails off to a flat-bottomed stern. Like John Goslee, he builds them by eye. The proportions and details are products of tradition, observation, conversation, trial and error, trial and success. There was a time when

Deadrise workboat, Taylor Island

he could have named fifteen other builders in the area, but most of them have died or quit, and he doesn't know how many are left—except that it is not many.

"First time I built a boat, a friend persuaded me to do it," he says slowly. "I'd always built furniture as a hobby, anything you'd find in a house. I didn't know one earthly thing about boats. I picked it all up talking with watermen, looking at other boats." As he speaks, a white-faced black kitten rakes its claws on his trousers. His barn has also acquired a reputation for sheltering and birthing cats. Twelve feline apprentices share the premises with the master craftsman. They roam throughout the barn, some eating from a flat dish on a bandsaw table, others lying on the half-finished boat or walking its ramparts. He moves toward the boat and sits down on the keelson, pulling one leg up and over the massive beam, letting the other extend down to the floor. He talks about building boats, all the while gently pushing away with his thick hands the cats that venture too close.

Raye selects and cuts the lumber for the wooden boats himself.

On his land are fifty acres of woods, which have a few big trees left. He knows of a few more in the community, but most of the big trees have been logged off in the last ten years, and finding them is getting to be a problem. Like Goslee, Raye uses white cedar for his hulls. Most of the framing is white oak. The keelson is loblolly pine; the starter boards, what the ribs are attached to, are also pine.

"Cedar will swell only a small amount," he says. "It doesn't waterlog the way pine or cypress will. It doesn't shrink a great deal either. Cedar is highly rot resistant, but it's soft and weak, and it wears out if it is used on washboards with people tonging off it. They use mats to keep the boards from being gouged by the tongs and from wearing out. Pine swells a lot in water. In the summer, pine swells in a day or two. It takes longer in the winter. On a pine boat, the boards on the bottom can swell so tight that they create a corrugated or rippled effect. You have to leave a gap for swelling when you use pine, especially if the wood is dry. About a third of the boats around here are built entirely out of pine. I've never built a pine boat. Now, it seems like most people want a cedar boat. You pay three times as much for cedar, which you have to get from North Carolina, but there is no problem getting pine and oak."

For his keelson, which will measure about ten inches by twelve inches by forty-two feet, Raye usually looks for a pine about 100 feet high, with a diameter of about twenty-two to twenty-four inches at chest height. He doesn't need a keelson that heavy, because the keelson seldom goes bad in a boat, but that's the way watermen like it. He wants the keelson tree to be slightly curved, starting at about ten to twelve feet up. The keelson should have a hook or bend in it so that the boat will come up on top of the water rather than plow into it. For the side boards, he needs straight trees, without too many knots. Loose knots in the staves have to be bored out and plugged, or else the boat will eventually leak. "A few years ago," he says, "you hardly had any knots. Now, the quality of the wood is not as good, and it seems like you have more."

Raye avoids the leaning cedar trees because cedar wood under stress is heavy, harder wood, and it tends to break under the pressure of springing. Or it cracks when he saws it. Like Goslee, Raye is skeptical about oak. "People always lump the oaks together," he says. "There are four kinds of white oak on the Eastern Shore: the true highland white oak, the basket oak, swamp white oak, and the overcup oak, all grown on the lowlands. Steer clear of all the oaks except the true highland, which I use for framing. Highland white oak is brighter, less brown-looking than the lowland." He avoids pine trees that have conch on the side—it looks like a toadstool. It's a sign the tree has red heart, rotten wood inside. The heart of the wood turns into a red honeycomb, and the wood is so full of holes it starts to crumble. "I've built two boats without catching it. Had it in the staves on the bottom of the boat."

Once he selects his trees, Raye lumbers and planes them himself at a sawmill. The lumber for the boat now under construction was brought to him by the man who ordered the boat, but it was green, so it had to sit in his shed for eighteen months before he could use it.

When he is ready to build, he secures the keelson with a chain from the ceiling of his barn and starts working it, squaring it up, making rough cuts with a boat slick, which looks like the offspring of an axe and a plane. The boat he is building is to be forty-two feet long. "To go out in the Bay, you want thirty-eight-foot and more, plus at least twelve-foot width." He cuts the beam down some, fairs it off, and carves in a sweep of seven to fourteen inches about one-third of the way back from the bow. "Some people take a straight tree, block it in the center, anchor it, and pull a bend. That's not so good. Your hook should be forward of center, in the front one-third. Why? I don't know, to be truthful. I always heard if you can get it there, put it there. The rest of the boat back of the vee is flat-bottomed. The flatter the stern and the bottom, the faster the boat will run. A lot of vee makes the boat run smooth. Too little vee makes it hit the seas rather than slice through them."

He next attaches the stem to the keelson. He has a plywood pattern for the stem and for the cabin window. Shaped like a swan's neck, the stem is white oak, one piece. He bolts it to the keelson using five eighteen-inch threaded stainless-steel rods. Once the stem is on, Raye can measure the amount of deadrise in the boat, which is seventeen inches, about average. Carried out the length of the boat, the bow will rise almost seventy-six inches above the floor of the barn; the stern, less than thirty-two inches.

So far, everything Raye has done has been upside-down. He builds the boat upside-down until the bottom is on. He mounts two pine side boards, one on each side, single planks of lumber measuring 1¼ inches by 12 inches by 43 feet, securing them first to the stem with stainless-steel nails. He puts in the pine chines (where bottom and side meet) on the inside of the starter boards, bending them around the shape of the boat. They help to form the intersection between the side and the bottom of a vee-bottomed boat. "The chine," he says, "gives you more area to attach the bottom to when you're putting on the bottom staves. Rather than having just 1¼ inches thick, you now have 2½ inches with the chines."

The stern is made of mahogany, three wide pieces glued together, measuring 1¾ inches by 10 inches by 11 feet for the average boat. He fastens them to the end of the keelson and to the sides. With the boat still upside-down, he builds the skeg, into which the alley for the propeller shaft will be bored. He attaches a wormstrake, a piece of oak to protect the skeg if it runs aground. "The skeg is pine," he says. "It's under water all the time. Anything completely submerged won't deteriorate. The salt water helps preserve the wood to some extent. Rainwater rots the wood. You have to use a wooden boat regularly or it goes bad."

The next step is to put on the bottom planking, starting at the

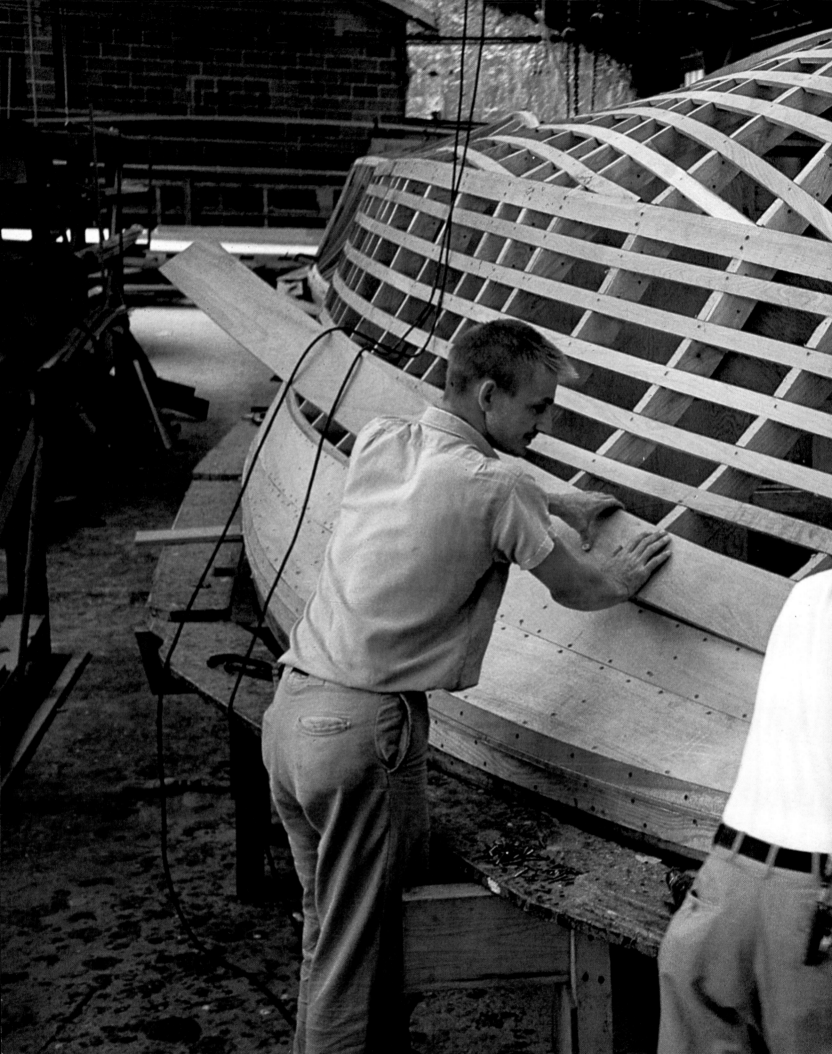

stern and progressing toward the bow. Raye used to put the planks on herringbone-style, swept back. "There was no point in it, so I quit it," he says. "I put 'em on straight across." The planks run lengthwise in the bow for about one-third of the boat; the remaining planks run across the boat, from side to side. The framing timbers in the bow are like studs in a house, places to nail the bow planking. Raye steams the bow planks so he can twist them to the shape he needs. To do this, he immerses the boards in a tank of boiling water for twenty to thirty minutes and fastens them while they're hot, because they are easier to bend and less likely to split or crack later on. To hold the bottom staves in place and force the right shape, he attaches bilge stringers, two to a side, pieces of lumber 3 inches by 3 inches by 28 inches that don't run the length of the boat. He then paints the bottom and prepares to turn the boat over.

"Turning over the first ten boats—I really dreaded that," he recalls. "Every board or piece is attached to the chine, and if you drop the boat on its side, you bust the chine, 'cause all that weight is borne by the chine. I know a fellow who regularly drops his boats when he turns them and has cracked the chine two or three times. I don't want to think about it. I don't know what I'd do. I used to get thirty or more people to help me turn it by hand." Now, he attaches a cable to a hole in the stern and one in the keelson and winches it up a few inches off the floor. He will stand on it and jump up and down to make sure nothing is going to give way before he lifts it up. Once he's certain, he raises it, then rotates it like a piece of meat on a spit.

Raye takes about five weeks to do the bottom, working alone twelve hours a day, six days a week. "I won't lie to you, but there was a time when I did three boats a year, one after the other, working seventy-hour weeks on the average, and sometimes as many as 100 hours a week. When I get in this building, I close the doors and forget about everything."

After he turns over the boat, he puts on ribs, sides, and six strongbacks, heavy cross beams of white oak, four by eight feet, which strengthen the boat. In Raye's opinion, they are a bit on the heavy side, not really necessary, but this is another example of where watermen follow tradition, wanting the same kind of boats their fathers or friends had. Into the boat goes still more fortification: the knees, upright pieces fastened to the strongbacks, which then fasten to the keelson at intervals of five feet. He puts on the washboards, the bow deck, and the stern deck. All are of white cedar and all go in together. What was a vision in his mind has become the shape of a real boat.

He planks in the bow with white cedar, boiling the gunwales or planks that bind in the top work, and covering the heads of the side timbers so that he can bend them to conform with the sweep of the boat. He constructs the cabin and pilothouse, but he doesn't like working inside the cabin. He has tried to get away from varnishing and customizing, and he seldom installs the engine, although he will help.

He doesn't want to say how much he charges for all of this, except that it's more than $13,000 (with no engine)—but it's a lot less than a fellow up in Cambridge whom he's heard charges on the high side of $20,000 for the same boat. In what may count as the understatement of the year on the Eastern Shore, Raye is less interested in publicity than his northern neighbor John Goslee. For one, he is terribly shy and uncomfortable talking about himself. Although newspaper reporters repeatedly have tried to interview him, he has never talked publicly about his hobby and has no plans to do so again anytime soon. And, unlike Goslee, he has people lined up waiting for boats. He'll talk prices with them, but that's business. "I think stuff like that is more or less private," he says. "I tell you the truth; I was always taught you never say how much you made. I'm going to change my prices anyway.

"If you can tell 'em you'll have 'em a boat in under six months, they'll give you money on it. I ask for $500. I want the rest when I get done. I don't want any money for something I haven't done. A lot of people want a boat yesterday. Within a few months, people start coming around. 'When you going to finish?' they ask. I used to build three boats in a year, then I did two. Now I'm going to one. It's too much work to build three in a year."

A man working seventy to 100 hours a week on a boat as a hobby has to have the right job. As one of 1,200 or 1,300 growers for Perdue Farms, Inc., of Salisbury, the nation's fifth-largest poultry producer, George Raye has a job that doesn't get in the way of his hobby too often. He doesn't have to spend much more time tending chickens than he does eating dinner and watching the evening news. It's the nature of the business. Perdue and the other poultry companies have taken just about everything except the smell out of the work of tending chickens. And Raye has even gotten used to that.

Without the chickens, boatbuilding for an independent operator like Raye would be a precarious existence. As the craft of boatbuilding heads the way of the dinosaur, embodying the age-old virtues of self-reliance and independence, the chicken business is heading for glory. Poultry is the Eastern Shore's number-one crop, ahead of corn and soybeans. Sussex County, Delaware, where Raye lives, is the largest poultry-producing county in the United States. So many people want chicken that the three Perdue processing plants on the Eastern Shore can't keep up. And it's not some regional peculiarity. Since 1960, when Americans ate an average of 27.8 pounds of poultry per person, consumption has grown to almost seventy pounds per person, with no end in sight as people continue to eat less beef and to try new products like chicken hot dogs and chicken bologna. Perdue alone sells more than 5 million chickens a week.

While Frank Perdue, the firm's owner, hawks chicken on television,

newspaper ads regularly profile successful growers who talk about the benefits of producing chickens for Perdue and encourage others to join them. They include bankers, farmers, librarians, firemen, housewives—people looking for second incomes as well as retirees who have found second careers as "chicken producers," the title Perdue gives to its network of growers. Company officials claim women make the best growers because they pay more attention to detail. Whoever they are and wherever they come from, they don't need a farm, just a single acre on which to build a chicken house, good for as many as 25,000 chickens. And, as Perdue points out, it takes a whole acre just to graze a single steer or two.

Roasters arrive at Raye's farm as one-day-old chicks. From a chicken's point of view, it is better to be a roaster than a broiler or a Cornish hen. Roasters remain at the farm for eleven or twelve weeks. Broilers depart after seven weeks; Cornish hens, after five weeks. The chickens spend most of their time eating and resting and remaining calm, so that when the Perdue agent shows up once or twice weekly to check their health and weight, they'll be on schedule. It is Raye's job to make sure nothing keeps his chickens from gaining weight on schedule.

The chicks have already been vaccinated and debeaked—the nerve in the beak is cauterized so the beak can't be used to inflict harm on other chickens. They are segregated by sex, temporarily partitioned into three groups in the chicken house, and watched closely. A flock of chickens is much more fragile than a herd of dairy cattle. A virus can wipe out an entire flock before the farmer is even aware of the extent of the problem. As a result, farmers are particular about whom they let near the chicken houses. Some even restrict vehicles from approaching too close, fearing they might bring in some disease on their tires. In the summer, mortality goes up because chickens are stressed by heat. They respirate through their mouths, and, stuffed into coops en route to market, they die easily on a hot, humid day. At the Perdue plant in Salisbury, fans the size of airplane propellers generate a steady flow of cool air over the trucks waiting to unload their live cargo. Even exercising normal precautions, about 1,000 of the 32,000 chicks that come to Raye's farm will die by the end of the growing period, a standard mortality rate.

Each chicken has been allocated four-fifths of a square foot in the design of the standard 40-foot-by-500-foot wood-and-galvanized-steel house. After the chicks begin to grow, the partitions come down and, theoretically, they have the run of the entire place. However, as they grow larger, they take up more and more of their square footage until finally, shortly before they depart, the floor of the house is a wall-to-wall shag carpet of fat, live chickens. Feed is supplied with an automatic conveyor belt that runs from a silo into which Frank Perdue delivers his special natural feed of soybean meal, imported Chilean anchovies, corn gluten, yellow cornmeal, and an extract of marigold petals. Perdue supplies the chickens, the feed, and the expertise. The grower pays for the feed and supplies the house, water, electricity, and labor.

Each morning, Raye checks to make sure the feed lines aren't clogged. He dumps the water troughs to get rid of the shavings and feed that the chickens have knocked into the water, and adjusts the feed lines to the height of their backs. He wants the chickens to stretch for the feed—that way, they don't waste as much by knocking it out of the pans with their bills. That's one of the important little things he does to control costs and improve his chances of appearing on Perdue's weekly list of top ten producers. He kills the ''culls''—breaks the neck of any chicken likely to be rejected at the factory: small or crippled chickens, or birds that have gone blind from the ammonia given off by their manure. Young chickens are most susceptible to the fumes. Once blinded, they stop eating and drinking. They stand with their eyes closed and rub their eyes against their feathers. ''Years ago,'' says Raye, ''there used to be enough sawdust and shavings to allow a complete clean-out of litter between flocks. Now, because of the expanding industry, there isn't enough sawdust available, and you have to run a year on the same litter. You get rid of the ammonia with exhaust fans, but they also carry out the heat. You have to get enough ammonia out without losing too much heat.'' Chicks need a constant temperature of eighty-five degrees, seventy as mature birds. Depending on the weather, Raye opens or closes the shutters on windows and doors to the houses. Chickens spook easily. A thunderstorm can cause them to panic and ''stack up,'' or pile up on top of each other, smothering those on the bottom.

At the end of about eleven weeks, Raye's chickens are ready to leave. He has nothing to do with the live-haul crews, the men who gather the birds from the houses and coop them for the truck ride to the processing plant. ''Ship it or smell it'' is the prevailing motto at Perdue, and their trucks loaded with chickens move up and down Route 13 at all hours of the day, some 9 million miles in a single year. The transportation system is intricate. Although there is a processing plant in nearby Salisbury, Raye's roasters go to Georgetown, Delaware, for distribution because that's the destination for all roasters on the Delmarva Peninsula. No Perdue bird ever has to travel more than sixty miles to be processed, a convenient system that allows Perdue to claim that chickens collected from Raye's farm on a Tuesday morning will be on the store shelves by Wednesday.

The trucks leave chicken feathers all over the Eastern Shore, and sometimes they even leave live, very confused chickens. Perdue receives occasional letters from irate citizens complaining about seeing whole chickens sitting stunned by the side of a highway, the ignoble end of an effort to squeeze through the hole of a coop in transit.

After the chickens have left, during the one-week interval before the next flock arrives, the houses have to be cleaned. The farmer who

Eastern Shore

leases Raye's cropland does the cleaning so he can have the manure for his fields. Perdue officials refer to chicken litter as ''gold'' because of its value as fertilizer. Horses and cows have nothing on chickens when it comes to potency of manure as fertilizer. But the addition of yet another rich source of fertilizer for the lands around the Bay has also made chickens major culprits in the problems of nutrient pollution.

What do Perdue chickens do for George Raye besides help to subsidize his boatbuilding? He gets paid according to a formula for feed conversion, how much weight the bird gains minus the cost of the feed. Raye averages about twenty-five cents revenue per bird, or about $32,000 per year on a turnover of four flocks—a nice sum for what averages out to about ninety minutes' work over the course of a day.

Feathers, trucks crammed with chickens, chicken houses galore— all are testimony to the prevalent role of the feathered creatures on the Delmarva Peninsula, where crop farming has been affected by the same ills that plague farming throughout the rest of the country. Raye long ago quit raising crops because there was no money in it. The value

Overleaf: *Worcester County*

of his farm has dropped to half of what it was ten years ago. It would be even worse if the farmers were not able to sell corn and soybeans for chicken feed. Perdue alone uses more than 45 million bushels of corn and crushes over 15 million bushels of soybeans a year.

Perdue offers the promise of a more secure future to farmers like Raye who switch from crop farming to producing chickens, but there's a trade-off. The farmer becomes another part of an automated assembly line of chicken production, a system so thoroughly analyzed and calculated down to the ounce, the second, the penny, that real diversity or independence is discouraged, if not eliminated, in favor of efficiency and profit. Like McDonald's and Kentucky Fried Chicken, Perdue, with its fleet of trucks, has become a symbol of yet another form of homogenization occurring on the Eastern Shore.

Note: George Raye is a fictitious name, based on a real person. While his friends will easily recognize his true identity, his name was changed to minimize any discomfort he felt in talking about himself.

A Matter of Context

*I*f Tom Horton were to fall over the side of his boat into the Chesapeake Bay, there are some people, especially on the Lower Eastern Shore, who would look the other way. It's not that they have anything personal against him. It's the fact that he's an environmentalist. They regard environmentalists as troublemakers—as people categorically opposed to all development, regardless of the economic needs of the region. And it's also the fact that he lives in Baltimore, where he writes for the *Baltimore Sun*. They see Baltimore and the Upper Bay as the source of all the problems of the Bay. Thus, he is tainted by association.

Horton is not from Baltimore, although he has lived there most of the time since 1963. In fact, he vows he will never say he is from Baltimore. He is from the Eastern Shore, from Federalsburg on Marshyhope Creek, and he has worked for the *Sun* since 1972. For several years, he has written a biweekly column entitled "On Environment," in which, at one time or another, he has taken issue with federal, state, and county governments, business and developers, industry, watermen, sportfishermen, the Upper Bay, the Lower Bay, the general public—all of whom he considers, with missionary zeal, to be in dire need of continuing education and guidance on matters of the environment. He is probably the most prominent environmental writer in the Chesapeake Bay area.

Horton had been invited on a boat trip one August day with a small group of people, some of whom participate as volunteers in various efforts to protect natural areas threatened by development. The boat, owned by John Warren, a retired regional administrator for the Department of Natural Resources, was to leave Shad Landing in Pocomoke River State Park and travel down the Pocomoke River to the town of Pocomoke. The party, complete with a home-baked feast, had the appearance of a summer outing, but it was mainly intended to provide a forum for Horton to talk broadbrush about the problems of the Chesapeake Bay, with specific reference to the Lower Eastern Shore. Although the entire trip took place in Worcester County, the focus of discussion was Somerset County, to the east.

Warren's small Cunard, named *The Pleiades II*, a double-decked cabin cruiser almost as broad of beam as the river, exceeded Horton's rather straightforward standard for messing about in boats: The boat must be "utterly simple," he had once written. "You cannot enjoy peace of mind in something featuring pleated vinyl and shag carpeting and deeply gleaming gelcoat finish and chrome, the kind of boat that sports a plaque saying, WELCOME ABOARD—REMOVE SHOES." Warren's boat lacked such "amenities," although its wood and brass surfaces gleamed brightly and reflected the loving care bestowed on it by the seventy-seven-year-old captain and his two older sisters, Elizabeth (who supervises the galley) and Josephine (who serves as first mate and brooks no interference from well-meaning passengers).

The trip afforded Horton a luxury he is altogether unaccustomed

Smith Island

to as a journalist, although he owns a nineteen-foot well-used skiff that he employs on his favorite river, the Nanticoke. He wasted no time adapting to the comfortable role of passenger, observer, and commentator.

"I believe the Pocomoke is the deepest river for its width in North America," he said, looking at the banks lined with cypress trees, which turn the color of cinnamon in the fall. One of the most scenic rivers in the east, its upper reaches lead to cypress swamps, while its lower reaches course through marshland into Pocomoke Sound.

A "people's bay" is what former Maryland governor Harry Hughes called the Chesapeake. It is hard to imagine a place, Horton once wrote, "where the water twines more intimately with the land in dozens of rivers and thousands of creeks; where the depths are as moderate, the tides as minimal, the sea heights as kindly; where these and a dozen other factors conspire half so well to create water so eminently usable for so many purposes by such large populations. And use it we have."

Overleaf: *Smith Island*

Horton's columns have dealt repeatedly with the theme of the Bay as a microcosm, an intense battleground, where everyone wants to live around the water and have the pleasure of water. "The paradox is that wherever modern man has settled next to rivers and streams and bays and lakes, next to the liquid edges that seem innately to draw him, the water quality inevitably has gone down roughly proportional to the rise in populations."

For a long time, sewage and industrial discharge had been the biggest problems connected with rising population, but by the 1970s it had become clear that there were other sources of pollution besides just what was "coming out of the ends of pipes."

"Following a natural human impulse to have three acres with mobile home and a place to dump oil," said Horton, projecting his voice above the noise of the boat, "there's been so much sprawling, unplanned development, the countryside is all hacked up. The Bay has been polluted with sediment runoff from lands that have been scalped of their topsoil by development and cleared of all forests."

The Eastern Shore was different agriculturally when Horton was a boy in Federalsburg. There was a lot of truck farming, with crops such as tomatoes, strawberries, and orchids. Now it's soybeans and corn, the main ingredients for the poultry farms that constitute the basis of the economy for the Delmarva Peninsula. Consequently, the farmer has become as big a culprit as the developer in the loss of forest. "Between 1960 and 1972, one county cut more than forty percent of its forests," said Horton. "Maryland had the highest forest loss rates in the Northeast in the 1960s and 70s. How bad the environment has gotten depends on your base line. People unfamiliar with the Eastern Shore say it looks bucolic. It does look bucolic, but I can see that where there used to be forest, now it's clearcut for soybeans."

In his columns Horton has lamented America's traditional dependence on a heavy meat diet, which exacts a price from land, water, and energy resources that "no country can afford to pay indefinitely." Two-thirds of all cropland in this country is devoted to growing feed for the animals "whose meat we eat and whose milk we drink. . . . A single acre of most grains or vegetables supplies the same amount of virtually every nutrient we need, where it requires ten to twenty-five acres to produce enough feed converted to beef. In other words, meat-eating in any form uses lots of extra land."

"There's too much nutrient runoff," said Horton, continuing his list of megaproblems, "principally nitrogen and phosphorus from sewage plants, and—the vast majority of it—from the heavy fertilization of cropland. Lancaster County in Pennsylvania has the highest density of farm animal population of any county in the country—produces 11 billion pounds of manure a year, far more than can be utilized by plants. We end up fertilizing the Bay as well."

Eastern Shore

Headquartered in Annapolis, the Chesapeake Bay Foundation, a private organization with 40,000 members founded more than twenty years ago to save the Bay, has a map of "nutrient enrichment for the Bay." The color red shows the heaviest, overrich concentrations of nutrients, and it spreads like a terrible cancer down the Upper Bay to Tangier Sound and west to the Rappahannock River. All of Tangier Sound westward is pink shading to dark red. The James is all red. The Pocomoke is all red; the Nanticoke, all red; the Potomac, the Patuxent, the Patapsco, and the Norfolk area—all red.

Nutrients promote the growth of algae in such quantities that it remains uneaten and unused, and in time it sinks to the bottom, where it rots, using up oxygen needed by other plants and by fish, turning the water anoxic—pathologically deficient of oxygen. The volume of anoxic water in the Bay has increased fifteen-fold in the last three decades. As the volume of anoxic water increases, winds slosh it out of its deeper depths. Totally anoxic water now appears in depths of seven to eight meters in the main stem of the Bay. As a result, the Bay is shrinking as

City Harbor, Annapolis

a habitat. Oysters used to be able to live at thirty feet; now their habitat has shrunk to depths of eighteen to twenty feet.

Horton cited other forms of pollution coming into the Bay: chemicals from auto tires, exhausts that run off paved urban surfaces, and enormous quantities of toxic metals. "Aberdeen Proving Ground," he said, "has been experimenting with chemicals and explosives for years, and there's evidence that the stuff is leaking into the Bay. The long-term effects aren't known. It's true that there's another side—there are 10,000 acres at Aberdeen that would have been developed by now. I once counted ninety-seven bald eagles nesting among the howitzers.

"We're moving now toward a more regulated situation to accommodate the increased numbers of people and preserve natural resources," said Horton. "Can't do it without regulation. It now requires a great amount of paper to hunt or fish, but more is coming, like driver's licenses for boats. The recently enacted Critical Areas legislation is another example. I think, hope, the attitude is changing from, 'We should develop areas the right way' to, 'There are some areas we just shouldn't develop.' "

Horton had made his introductory comments from the top deck of

Tom Horton

the boat, facing the stern. He had spread his arms aloft over the edge of the canvas roof, which he could reach because he is six feet five inches tall. Pictures of him sitting in a canoe show three discernible human shapes: Horton in the stern, a friend in the bow, and, almost amidships, Horton's knees projecting skyward.

When he walks, Horton appears to lunge from one foot to the other, as if he had a basketball in hand and was about to lay it up against the backboard, which he did for a while as a center for Johns Hopkins University in Baltimore before retiring after knee surgery. He graduated with a degree in economics in 1968 and spent the following four years in Ethiopia as an Arabic translator for the U.S. Army. He wears horn-rimmed glasses, and his dark brown hair seems permanently windblown.

Horton is supremely happy about having grown up in Federalsburg, a town of about 3,000 people. His boyhood during the 1950s now seems idyllic, a Norman Rockwell sampler of life on the Chesapeake when the Bay was more bountiful and there were fewer people. The Bay Bridge was just being completed in 1954, and it was well before Ocean City

Overleaf: *Annapolis*

would start to boom. It was a time when natural resources seemed limitless, and fish and wildlife were there for the taking—in quantities that seem excessive today. Strangely enough, he can remember that aspect of his fishing and hunting without remorse. Times were different, as were levels of awareness.

Growing up in a small town, Horton had a lot of free time. He played in the woods, in streams, in boats on the open water. He developed a strong affection for dirt roads, walking on them barefooted, following them on their often lonely journeys through the woods and backcountry of rural life. He remembers Marshyhope Creek being red with tomato peels and chicken guts and yellow with chicken feet from processing plants that flushed their renderings into the nearest local waterway, but the water was still so unimpacted compared to today that the fishing was great.

"I can remember my father hunting around Hooper Island and coming back with 100-pound burlap sacks full of canvasback and redhead ducks," he said. "Dozens and dozens of ducks and geese. It was nothing for me to pick up thirty or forty black ducks, fifteen geese in a single night. We had duck hunting you couldn't buy today. They seemed inexhaustible. Now, they may not be around in the twenty-first century because of both overhunting and habitat degradation. Rockfish, our bread-and-butter fish, we used to catch by the dozens, occasionally by the hundreds. I remember rockfish fighting in the rivers, thrashing in the shallows on Nanticoke on their spawning run, so many of them they made an enormous noise. I never really understood much about herring, which I'd catch by the hundreds and throw half away." They fished the gravel pits near Federalsburg for the crappies that spawned there, coming in on high tide from the river, and for bullfrogs, catching them on the edges of the ponds at night to sell.

On vacations or weekends, Horton's mother and two sisters would head for the beach; Tom and his dad would take off for the Honga River, off Hooper Island, where his father's poultry plant owned land and a hunting lodge. He loved the special atmosphere of the retreat, although his father now says that if fumes from alcohol and cigars could kill, his son never would have survived that special atmosphere.

One of their frequent hunting companions was a waterman named Ackley Tyler, who helped Horton refine his hunting and fishing skills. As Horton got older, he spent Christmas vacations with him, breaking every game law in existence. His education as a young environmentalist included trapping or shooting raccoon, muskrat, geese, ducks, and deer, not to mention fish, oysters, and soft- and hard-shell crabs. He even learned to hunt under extreme duress. It was time to go goose hunting one year and he was still on crutches, suffering from the first of three knee operations. His father can remember his son hobbling across the marshes on crutches after a goose he'd shot. One November, near Thanksgiving, they went goose hunting, caught rockfish and oysters, ate crab soup, and fried soft crabs—they ate everything the Bay offered in a single meal. "The amazing thing is that today, in a diminished way, we could still come close to equaling that," said Horton.

Horton had retired to a padded bench along the top deck, where he sat with one leg folded over the other, his shirtsleeves rolled up, two sticks of gum in his mouth. The wake of the boat rushed both banks of the narrow river, crashing over the lily pads. Channel markers bobbed up and down.

"Somerset County," he said, "is one of the last great places with wetlands. Somerset and Dorchester counties have about three-quarters of all the wetlands in the state. About one-quarter—63,000 acres—of Somerset's land surface is wetlands. People in the Upper Bay, in places like Anne Arundel County—the most heavily developed part of the Bay—want to keep it that way."

His many opponents on the Lower Eastern Shore have objected to the implicit "elitism" in that attitude, arguing that Horton assumes that places like Somerset County would make the same mistakes as the Upper Bay in determining the fate of their wetlands. And besides, they point out, the Upper Bay is the source of the Chesapeake's pollution anyway.

"If you follow that reasoning," replied Horton, "now that we know better, given Baltimore's past history, should we not do anything but stand by and watch others repeat our mistakes? There's proof that Kent Island, the eastern terminus of the Bay Bridge, is well on its way to making the same stupid mistakes. The problem is we can't wait to see the threat. When you ride up the river and say, 'Jesus, it's starting to go,' it's gone. Kent Island is growing houses now, but the seeds were planted thirty years ago. Thirty years from now, the same Kent Island developers will be coming into Somerset County. Preserving wetlands translates into preserving seafood and water quality.

"The Susquehanna River [in the Upper Bay] is a major source of pollution," said Horton. "But for the idea that watermen have that if you get Baltimore out of the Bay, the water would be OK, that's just not so. You could take Baltimore off the map and it still would not affect the Upper Bay. Baltimore's main sewage plant flushes into Back River, the most poorly flushed in the Baltimore river system. The Back River has a feeble circulation and acts as a sink, as tertiary treatment. The impact is far less than if you'd put it into the Bay."

By far the major issue of contention between residents of areas like Somerset County and the environmentalists is how much of the wetlands to preserve. Horton's opponents are vehement in their belief that not all wetlands development is negative.

"I don't think environmentalists and land developers are ever going to have a happy marriage. But because of the environmentalists, over the next ten years we're going to spend billions of dollars to clean up sewage; hire lots of new people to help with the problems of farm runoff. Because of the environmentalists, the Save the Bay package passed. It's incredible the efforts of the environmentalists didn't work

Kent Island

for Somerset County, but it doesn't exactly hurt the county, either. It's not a negative. Somerset will be better off if rockfish, oysters, and aquatic grass can be brought back.'' Horton was referring to the most significant casualties to date of Bay pollution, the drastic decline of the oyster industry from overharvesting and disease wrought by pollution, the state ban on rockfishing, and the loss, over the last five years, of eight-five to ninety percent of the Bay's underwater grasses, which are essential to underwater life.

Somerset County and the Lower Eastern Shore have a difficult time influencing legislation because they lack political clout. The Maryland Senate and House are apportioned on the basis of one man/one vote. The Eastern Shore has only one senator for the whole Lower Shore — Somerset, Wicomico, and Worcester counties. As a result, the Lower Eastern Shore is consistently outvoted and their legislators have to wheel and deal with other legislators, or they won't get any political support at all. ''The power is in the developed areas,'' says one Somerset County resident. ''They can pass anything they want. Yet pollution and destruction of the Bay continues.''

Somerset County residents see the recently enacted Critical Areas legislation as an example of how the political process seems to work to their disadvantage. Opponents fail to see how the density regulation will significantly reduce water pollution, since they believe the major pollution sources come from industry, sewage, and farm runoff up the Bay. Somerset County seems unlikely to enforce Critical Areas legislation until it is forced to do so.

"They're right," said Horton. "That's a good point—the rich get richer. People in Anne Arundel County say, 'Preserve the Eastern Shore,' while they cut down 100 acres of trees in Fishing Creek. I don't have any comeback to that. It wasn't equitable—it was political. So much about the Chesapeake Bay is decided in the sixteen to eighteen different counties, by different bodies of elected officials holding radically different opinions. It's not OK. It just is. It's deplorable; so many pork barrels. But chances are likely that if I had been running the government, or anyone else had, we'd have had to do it the same way.

"The Critical Areas laws were constructed to preserve wildlife habitat," said Horton. "It's pretty radical to restrict private use of land for aesthetics. It's not been done in many places. If the far-reaching effect had been explained to the legislature, it never would have passed. I don't think housing density makes a hoot of difference on traditional water pollution. But, in other areas, it's a pretty damned radical law. In Somerset County, if they dig in their heels and resort to courts, the Critical Areas laws won't work. Somerset County—even though it doesn't have much power—can't take the attitude, 'Take it and lump it.'

"I'd be willing to admit," he continued, "that environmentalists haven't shown sensitivity to economic needs. A lot of prejudice and stereotyping go on on both sides. Every politician says he's for the environment. The only hope for reconciliation between environmentalists and the Eastern Shore is some kind of give-and-take."

Give-and-take is not likely as long as areas like Somerset County see environmentalists as being unequivocally opposed to development everywhere. When a plan is proposed for development, environmentalists "go crazy," as one resident of Crisfield describes it. Thus, while no further development is allowed unless the environment can be protected, it is almost impossible to get that input. "It's the tragedy of today," says Laura Ritter, editor of *The Crisfield Times*. "Instead of joining to develop creative solutions that could be model plans for other communities facing the same problems, environmentalists and developers don't talk to each other."

Route 413, a two-lane spur in Somerset County, leads southwest from Route 13 down the peninsula to the bayside port of Crisfield. The road is so straight that one car can begin to pass another when it's still a quarter-mile behind, ride the left lane, and see three miles ahead to where the heat waves reflect off the macadam in the summer,

Overleaf: *Crisfield*

transforming it into mirror glass and doubling the image of the next car ahead. Somerset County is a place where too many people walk along the shoulders of the roads because they don't own cars, or because they've been apprehended while driving drunk and lost their licenses. It's the place with the lowest per-capita income in the state, twelve or thirteen percent annual unemployment, and only two towns of any size—Princess Anne and Crisfield. Crisfield is caught in a dilemma, and its survival may be at stake.

Buses full of tourists from cities up and down the Atlantic Coast arrive in Crisfield almost daily during the summer, heading for Smith and Tangier islands, where they take a short tour and eat a seafood meal. When they return the same day, they get right back on the buses and leave, having spent no money in Crisfield. Ideas are at a premium as to how to detour them into Crisfield for a few hours, even overnight. The only beaches are immediately adjacent to marshland. In the hottest months of the year, the waters fill with sea nettles. Crisfield has a museum with local memorabilia, some new restaurants, a few new gift shops, and, for those with boats, a marina with a swimming pool. But it lacks the boutiques and the studied cuteness that apparently help to attract crowds of tourists to such areas as Annapolis. The town and the rest of Somerset County seem to be making some gains in promoting tourism. (The county's most recent pertinent figures—for 1985—show tourist spending up eighteen percent over the previous year, but tourism still is an improving industry.)

Route 413 runs beside the abandoned railroad bed that once carried long trains of seafood produce from Crisfield to Salisbury, where it was shipped to restaurants in the Northeast for their many patrons who savored and insisted upon the Maryland oyster. The railroad and the oyster made Crisfield. At the turn of the century, Crisfield had as many as seventy-five oyster-shucking houses, fifty crab-packing plants, four theaters, three bowling alleys, three or four dance halls, and twenty-five barbers. When the oyster shuckers came to town, the population of 3,000 to 5,000 swelled to 15,000. Oyster shells were piled as high as telephone poles.

The town is on a low peninsula formed by Tangier Sound to the west, Pocomoke Sound to the south. In between, as if trying to pry apart and split the peninsula, is the Little Annemessex River. The encroaching sea has formed thousands of little islets and thousands of acres of marshland, which became a habitat for crabs, oysters, and fish, and for the early users of such bounty, the Indians. According to the compendium *History of Crisfield and Surrounding Areas on Maryland's Eastern Shore* (Gateway Press, Inc., Baltimore, 1974), by Woodrow T. Wilson, a Crisfielder, the Annemessex and Pocomoke Indians, tribes of the Algonquin Nation, settled in the region, giving it the name Annemessex, meaning "bountiful waters."

The majority of the white settlers who began arriving after 1660 came from Virginia's eastern shore, where the most valued land already was gone. On February 10, 1666, a parcel of land containing 300 acres in "Emmesox" was surveyed for Benjamin Summers, and soon there was a fishing village at "Somers" Cove. Many of its original buildings were supported by stilts. The land around them was filled with oyster shells.

It was a region also filled—in the words of an English visitor in 1742—with "vermin of various sorts and sizes, cats, dogs, convicts, bugs, musketoes [sic], worms of every sort both land and water, spiders, snakes, hornets, wasps, sea nettles, ticks, gnats, thunger [sic] and lightning, excessive heat, excessive cold, and other irregularities in abundance."

By 1807, Crisfield had more than 100 buildings, compared to Princess Anne with forty and Salisbury with only four. The Revolutionary War and the War of 1812 barely touched Crisfield, the closest fighting taking place in 1812 at the Battle of Jenkins Creek, against British soldiers who were garrisoned at Tangier Island. Through most of the period before the Civil War, Chesapeake Bay schooners engaged in a prosperous trade with Crisfield, taking on wheat, corn, tobacco, and cotton from the surrounding farms.

Just before the Civil War, a resident of Norfolk appeared in Somers Cove with his boat and a pile of oysters, which he showed some local fishermen how to shuck faster than they were used to. He then sailed his cargo of fresh oysters up to Baltimore, sold them, and returned for more. In a few years, hundreds of boats were engaged in the oyster trade on the Bay. The result was a boom in the fortunes of Crisfield, which soon proclaimed itself the Seafood Capital of the World. Trains had their boxcars filled full of oysters and crabs and shad from the skipjacks that crowded the harbor in such numbers that it was possible to walk across them from one side of the harbor to the other. One hundred carloads of seafood per week left town during peak season. On one day, December 19, 1920, a train left for Salisbury with eighteen carloads of oysters. By 1910, Crisfield had become such an important port of entry that its customs house had the largest registry of sailing vessels of any American port.

Trade and passenger travel was almost exclusively by water until 1866, after the Civil War, when entrepreneurs brought the railroad to Crisfield, building it to within one mile of the water's edge. An attorney named John Woodland Crisfield, who lived in Princess Anne at the time and was counsel for the principal supporters of the railroad, was instrumental in completing the project. In appreciation, the town changed its name from Somers Cove to Crisfield. The town began to grow rapidly, and a decision was made to extend the railroad to the water's edge, and, in a second stage, to Old Island to develop a deepwater seaport. The first stage of track was built in 1867 on piling

Overleaf: *Tom Ward at his barbershop, Crisfield*

and trestles to the end of a wharf that now has been converted to a big, open deck with a roof and benches. It's known as "the Depot." The surrounding area was filled to track level with oyster shells. The second stage was eventually abandoned because of expense and because of opposition from the seafood-packing plants, whose management feared that a seaport would draw industry that would compete for the cheap labor. Gradually, Crisfield, regurgitating oyster shells as fast they came in, grew outward toward the area of the Depot. Today, the area around the Depot has the landscape of a coral atoll. Except for a handful of lonely saplings in the Main Street median strip where the railroad once ran, there are few trees beyond the old downtown area that surrounds the post office.

When Tom Ward used to open his barbershop at six in the morning fifty and sixty years ago, he often as not had to step over drunks from the gambling boats who had passed out on his doorstep. Another six or seven would be roused out of the town jail, where they had spent the night for fighting. There were a half-dozen speakeasies ("raw bars," they called them) with such names as Teapot Dome, Bucket of Blood, Sailor's Horn. The boat crews and the shuckers gave Crisfield a reputation for drinking, fighting, and lawlessness that spread beyond the town boundaries. Taverns up the peninsula posted signs saying, NO CRISFIELDERS ALLOWED. In those days, Tom was one of twenty-five barbers in town. Now there are three, and Tom spends a lot of his time slouched in one of his chairs, staring out at Main Street, talking with friends who stop in to pass the time of day.

A day in modern Crisfield unfolds against a background of confidence and pride in its past, in its ability to cope with nature, in the fact that it has produced a governor of Maryland, a president of the state university, five generals, and the founder of the Del Monte food corporation. At sunrise, the whole north side of Main Street catches fire. The contours of L. Forbush and Sons Hardware glow. Pruitt's custom canvas upholstery shop blazes like a fiery banner. At 6:24 a.m. on the electric clock above the Eastern Shore National Bank, the temperature is eighty degrees. J.P. Tawes of J.P. Tawes and Brothers Hardware, the third hardware store on the block, is open and selling ice to party boats. The *Captain Genze*, out of Stevensville, Maryland, is loaded with thirty fishermen at $20 each—men, women, boys, all black, going fishing for hardheads, trout, croakers, or spot. One man cuts up squid for bait with a long knife while he waits.

Halfway down Main Street, Gordon's Restaurant has been open since 4 a.m. Gordon's has a counter, some booths, and a few tables occupied by older watermen, those who have earned the right to eat a slow breakfast before they go out on the water. The air is thick with cigarette smoke and the sound and aroma of bacon and eggs frying. For $2, a visitor can get a bacon-and-egg sandwich that comes, as often as

Maryland Avenue, Crisfield

not, with a thumbprint. Gordon's has been here for sixty years and is entitled to its eccentricities, among which are two cigar boxes known locally as the "live box" and the "dead box." In them are pictures of the regular customers. When one dies, his picture is taken out of the live box and put in the dead box. According to legend, anyone who sits in a chair at Gordon's known as the "good-bye chair" is doomed to die very soon thereafter.

Out of the morning light comes the sound of a pickup truck traveling toward the Depot. The driver takes a U-turn in front of the Depot and pulls into the parking lot of the Captain's Galley Restaurant and Bar, once an old oyster-shucking house. "Buddy," says the driver to an early-morning observer, stepping out of his cab, lifting his cap with one hand and straightening his hair with the other, "When's this bar open up? I wanna beer and make a phone call." The bank clock reads 6:34 a.m.

Shortly after, a bench sitter appears on a faded bench outside

CAPTAIN
GEORGE
WILL BE
WHEN
BOAT
CAPT. GEORGE
STEVENSVILLE MD

Tawes. He is the first of a society of Depot sitters, most of them retirees, who spend a good part of their days sitting on wooden benches in the shade of the Depot, watching the harbor traffic and talking with each other.

Across the harbor, the crab-packing houses have been operating since well before dawn. There are about twenty seafood-packing houses left in the area, including John Handy Seafood, reputedly the largest soft-crab packer in the world. The crab pickers arrive in the dark in the early-morning hours. Later, the heat drives them out of their workrooms.

The temperature is in the mid-eighties by midmorning, heading for the low nineties. The mailboats to Smith and Tangier arrive with passengers and prepare for the return trips, departing shortly after noon. Other tourists linger at the Depot until they can board the tour boats across the harbor in Somers Cove Marina for the more leisurely but more expensive trip to the islands.

In late morning, the workboats begin to return with their day's catch of crabs, now the staple of Crisfield's fishing industry. They come into the harbor, one after the other, unloading at the different seafood plants that line one side of the harbor. As the Bay declines, their days grow longer. After they discharge their cargoes, they go off to work on their boats and prepare for the next day's fishing.

On a typical summer night, around 9 p.m., the U-turn at the end of Main Street, by the Depot, becomes a hangout for youngsters. Jeeps, pickup trucks, mudhoppers, dune buggies, rusting modified vans with throaty roars; vehicles with loud radios blaring rock and roll, or country and western, or country rock; girls with girls, girls with boys, boys with boys—all ride the median strip down one side of Main Street to the U-turn, up the other, and back again. Locals call it ''cruising the doughnut.'' The problems of being a teenager in Crisfield are the problems of chronic high employment, of a lack of role models, of few educational and cultural resources—no recreation hall and limited horizons. As one town resident comments, ''How do you motivate a sixteen-year-old in the tenth grade who earns enough money from crabbing to own three boats, insurance, and have money in the bank?''

Civic pride and the spirit of endeavor in Crisfield too often flag in the face of uncertainty and pessimism about the town's future. Some residents want economic well-being for the town, but they worry that Crisfield will turn into a ''baby Ocean City.'' Others say it is more likely to become a ghost town, because Crisfield and the county have ocean-size problems—a low, assessable tax base, for one. A one-cent tax increase generates only $5,000 to $6,000 more among the taxable in the county's population of 19,000. There is no middle class. Poorer people don't have the outlook, the perspective to change. As one observer

Overleaf: *Crisfield*

reports, "They come to interviews with no shirt on and ask what you pay. It's not just a black problem; it's a white problem, too. Older people don't want to change. They don't like the Bay Bridge or the Tunnel, even though those are the only two ways to get off the peninsula."

There is no discernible reason why industry should turn off Route 13 and travel down a cul-de-sac to Crisfield. And so it hasn't. There hasn't been any new industry in Crisfield in fifteen years. In the meantime, the garment factories—which once helped stabilize employment in Crisfield by hiring women whose income supplemented the more seasonal income of the watermen—are gone, the last one having closed in 1972. Mrs. Paul's Kitchens has a plant in Crisfield that packs fried clams, onion rings, sweet potatoes, and zucchini and eggplant sticks. And Rubberset makes paintbrushes at the edge of town, not too far from Carvel Hall, makers of steak and oyster knives and gift cutlery. But they are only remnants, incapable of providing in themselves a sound economic base for the town.

What Crisfield, the fading seafood capital of the world, has left is the water, and the fact that the town is a nice place to live—for retirees, and weekenders who don't have to depend on the local economy for jobs. Although the water no longer provides the same bounty it once did, people increasingly will come from all over to use the water, to live near the water, as evidenced by the faster-than-average increase in waterfront property values in Crisfield and throughout the county. Crisfield, of course, can no longer do as it pleases with the water. Development of water property around Crisfield means development of wetlands, which is banned in Maryland under a 1970 law. In 1986, an event occurred that seemed to epitomize the situation in which Crisfield and places like it find themselves as they seek options for the future in the face of an ever-increasing national effort to protect wetlands.

The event had to do with a proposal to build a maritime park in Crisfield that would create more year-round jobs for the town and expand the city's tax base. According to *The Crisfield Times*, the city had proposed to develop a maritime industrial park between Route 413 and the Little Annemessex River—more precisely, between Little Boat Harbor and the extended downtown section of Main Street, on the west side. It is an area covered mostly by marshland, though it is a site that once had been used for dredging soil and was not considered "quality marshland." The original plan had called for a barge offloading facility and a staging area that would provide public access to the water. Ultimately, some twenty-eight acres of wetlands would have been filled in and destroyed.

The Army Corps of Engineers, which is empowered to permit a development project if economic benefits seem likely to outweigh the environmental costs of wetlands destruction, had turned it down, contending that Crisfield lacked firm commitments from industry for

development of the area. Crisfield had argued in return that the town could not be expected to gain firm commitments for a waterfront industrial park until the park existed. The town believed the anticipated economic benefits for the future of Crisfield more than compensated for the minuscule loss of habitat in an area that, in the opinion of some, was already polluted. The city had revised its plan, but each time it did so, the Army engineers sent it back, asking for further information. It seemed to be a stalling tactic designed to exhaust the promoters of the venture. And exhausted they became, and discouraged, and bitter toward those like Tom Horton, who symbolized the opposition of environmentalists to the plan, and thus to the welfare of the city. They went back to the drawing boards to try yet again, but with no glimmer of hope that they would ever secure a permit.

Horton himself had opposed the plan. "I assure you," he said after a visit to the site, "that if Crisfield had been made an exception for wetlands development, other developers would use the precedent. Crisfield has a legitimate problem. It's caught in a national wetlands legislative movement. Marshes have gotten deified. You'd have to be Jesus Christ to get an OK to fill in twenty acres of salt marsh. Say you're the Environmental Protection Agency (EPA). How do you do it, case by case? I'd still argue that because some counties are irresponsible, you should have clamps on all wetlands development. Land developers are a bunch of avaricious greedheads. I don't like to link business with development. You get skewed results. A lot of business supports the environment. I don't say Crisfield and the state shouldn't get more involved in trying to figure out what to do. But there is great peril."

Still another problem of the type that regionally distinct communities like Crisfield face occurred in July 1986, when a man named Sanford Justice filed an application with the Somerset County Zoning Board to build a marina, an airstrip, and 200 two- and three-bedroom townhouses on Smith Island, twelve miles west of Crisfield. The island seemed like the last place anyone would want to develop, and the plan sent shock waves up and down the Bay.

Seen from a distance, Smith Island lacks the spectacular profile of a Pacific or Caribbean island. It is a thin, green line joining sky and water. More water than land, it is an archipelago of marsh, with low ridges and scattered clumps of trees cut by creeks and guts. High ground on Smith, which averages two feet above sea level, is scarce, occupied for the most part by the island's three towns; undeveloped high ground is scarcer, and Justice owns all of what is left of it.

Justice hardly seemed to fit Horton's description of developers as "avaricious greedheads." Until 1981, he was an elementary school librarian. That year, he was told he had asbestosis, so he retired early. With time on his hands, and farmland inherited from his wife's family to use for collateral, he had done little except think about developing the land around Pitchcroft, an old house on a point a short distance from the

Smith Island

dock in Ewell, on Smith. The house dates back to Revolutionary War days and was to be the centerpiece in his development until it burned to the ground in late fall last year. Justice purchased the house and ninety acres fourteen years ago for $40,000. He proposed to sell each of his townhouses for upward of $150,000.

Smith Islanders had started encouraging him to develop the property a few years earlier. " 'You know,' " he recalls them saying, " 'you've got all that land. Why don't you put cabins there?' I know people here want it, and that's why I'm doing it. There is no work here for the islanders the way it is now. Many are having to leave the island. My plan will provide something for women to do besides pick crabs. They'll clean the places and make some money. People coming here will bring money onto the island—that's the name of the game."

A kindly, avuncular man who is fifty-three years old, Justice worked assiduously over the years to cultivate the islanders' favor. He vacationed on Smith Island for many years and often invited children who were friends of his daughter's to accompany them on Christmas shopping trips north to stores like Wanamaker's in Philadelphia. Today, when he rides over to the island via one of the two boat companies that

Overleaf: *Smith Island*

transports passengers, he always returns with the other, making sure that both know what he is doing. He spreads his appetite evenly among the island's handful of small restaurants and inns. He has been glad to donate landfill for the fire department and the baseball diamond. Included in his plan is a swimming pool for the islanders, who cannot swim in their own waters after midsummer because of the infestation of sea nettles. He would institute an annual charge of $250 per townhouse owner for the Ewell Volunteer Fire Department, and he would provide garbage removal for the island, along with additional electrical power and new wells.

Justice had quickly withdrawn his first application so he could talk with islanders and get their input. After holding public meetings on the island, he eliminated the airstrip plan because the islanders were fearful of having airplanes landing over their homes. He scaled down the density of the housing to allow other island businessmen to utilize some of his sewage capacity. Despite his efforts, he was unable to overcome the disbelief, the suspicion, and—as may have been the case in the fire at Pitchcroft—the outright hostility.

"We'll have every sort and size, every color and creed, every

Smith Island

denomination in here," one islander said in reaction to the plan.
"It is ignorant. It makes me sick." Others worried about outsiders being
"dumped" on them, people who would be strictly weekend citizens,
wouldn't support anything, and would change the nature of the island.

"It's only talk," said one. "Justice hasn't ever done anything like
this. It's not real. It's not feasible. If you can't afford to build in
Crisfield, how can you afford it on Smith Island?"

"It's the biggest joke ever. . .," said another, adding, "J.R. Ewing
and Blake Carrington [from television's "Dallas" and "Dynasty"] are
the onliest ones who could do it."

"Sanford Justice told us there will be plenty of jobs," said Frances
Kitching, who owns a popular island restaurant and has written a
cookbook that she sells to tourists. "But in the summers, women on
the island already work in crabs, men work on the water. We don't need
jobs. In the winter, when women would be available to work, the wind
gets blowing, and the people just wouldn't like it here. A lot of people
comes here and wants to change things around, but people are set
in their ways. They have worked out what would be best for them."

Many islanders, like Gerald Tyler, a tugboat captain, saw the plan
as a way to gain important benefits, such as improved medical care, but
they were waiting to see in black and white what the plan entailed
before they decided. "We're not the type of people who change for
every fad," said Tyler. "Things have to be proved to us."

Justice's property is not wetlands; hence, his proposal did not
appear to violate existing wetlands protection laws. However, Somerset
County has a law in its zoning code that requires a developer to prove
his project will not have an adverse effect on the quality of life in the
existing area. Since there were no significant environmental issues,
the opposition focused on "the quality of life."

The fact that Justice or anyone else was planning a development
on Smith Island showed just how intense the pressures on the Bay
had become. Rapid population growth in the Washington-Baltimore-
Philadelphia corridor has had an impact on the Eastern Shore. As
Horton said, Kent Island has become one of the biggest boom areas in
Maryland. The commercial watermen's community, or what's left of it,
is hemmed in by townhouses and condominiums. Two other watermen's
communities, Rock Hall (once the center of rockfishing) and Tilghman
Island, are being similarly transformed.

Horton had written against Justice's plan, summing up his point
of view in this way: "Can you put sixty-two townhouses on an island
and basically double the population with people who are quite different
from the islanders and not affect them negatively? That has to be the
basis of any decision to proceed with the plan."

Stung by what he considered ignorant attacks on his plan, Justice
said Horton had let living in Baltimore go to his head. "What will my

Overleaf: *Smith Island*

development change?'' he asked. ''There will still be crab boats. I'm not putting New York City on the island. Some of those environmentalists want to keep Smith Islanders on display for tourists, as if they were caged animals, or barefoot and ignorant, so they will have more to write about. Smith Islanders are just like other people—if the islanders didn't want the project, more of them would have been at the meetings I held.''

The Crisfield Times had responded to the plan with an editorial by Laura Ritter that presented the larger problem:

> It may have been appropriate to drop this particular plan. A project as large and aggressive as this one somehow seemed to contradict the serene quality of island life.
>
> Local officials are to be commended for their attempt to hold a public hearing on the project on Smith Island. Planning such a hearing recognizes that the islanders will be significantly affected by development and that the people of Smith Island must be an integral part of any development process.
>
> What is clearly less commendable is the opposition to this proposal by every environmentalist from Ocean City to Baltimore. Instead of discussing the impact of the project on the fish and the sea grass, these self-appointed protectors of the watermen found it necessary to look out of their suburban picture windows and tell the big-city media what the people of Smith Island want and need. Calls even came in from New York, from a poor city fellow who was afraid of losing the charming island retreat he considers his own.
>
> The role of the environmentalists should be to defend and protect the natural environment; to present, for example, facts on how the proposed development will affect water quality or wildlife. This is an important role, and if it were done right, it would keep the environmentalist community so busy they wouldn't have time to look from afar and worry about the quaintness of a waterman's life.
>
> . . . [Smith Islanders] are also worldly enough to realize that nothing can ever stay the same; some growth is necessary to protect and continue the way of life they lead. . . .

Visitors walking along Smith Island's only road discover they are taller than anything they can see and that from almost any vantage point on the island, they can, as one islander describes it, ''see the sunrise and sunset all the way 'round.'' Set against an endless sweep of sky and water, the tawny, muted colors of the marsh change slowly, almost imperceptibly, with the seasons. The island has an aura of serenity about it that makes it seem far removed from the real world— which it is. Suburbia has yet to reach as far down the Eastern Shore as

Smith Island

Somerset County, of which Smith Island is nominally a part. Although it is only five hours by car and boat from the heart of the Northeast, Smith Island is economically and culturally a world apart, a unique community, one of the last in the Chesapeake region.

The sunflowers and goldenrod that greet a visitor in August are littered with broken appliances and tools and junked cars. Until last year, there were close to 600 cars on an island whose total highway system consists of a single two-lane road about two miles long. (Until recently, the road was a cheap composition of tar. On summer days, it softened so much that, on one occasion, it entrapped a frail island woman, who had to be rescued by two passing youths.) Most of the automotive fleet were corroding hulks abandoned where they had died. Because Smith Islanders steadfastly ignore such rites of government as annual car registration, none of the vehicles had license plates, and their owners were thus anonymous. The problem got so out of hand that islanders finally petitioned the state to dig a trench in the marsh and bury them. After much grousing and foot-dragging, the state finally agreed to do so, but not without warning the islanders that they would have to deal with the problem themselves next time. About 500 cars went into that watery grave, at a cost of $163,300 to the state's taxpayers.

The islanders are for the most part watermen, or commercial fishermen, whose names are those of their forefathers who settled the

Overleaf: *Smith Island*

island in 1657, just fifty years after it was first charted by Captain John Smith. For centuries, they have fished the rich estuaries of the Bay, first for oysters and later terrapin, as well as hard- and soft-shell crabs, becoming prime suppliers to markets in cities throughout the Northeast. They spend their daily life on the water, dependent on their instincts and their knowledge of the weather and tides to thwart the always dangerous Bay. They give the impression of being content with things as they are. Their easy fatalism derives in part from their devout faith that what will come is preordained.

There are no police officers, no familiar forms of government authority on the island. Ewell is the largest of the island's towns, one of which, Tylerton, is accessible only by boat. Some of the houses on Ewell's two narrow main streets resemble the white cottages that appear on postcards of Martha's Vineyard or Nantucket. Others are plain or ramshackle, some of them converted trailers. Four small grocery stores, where watermen play dominoes during bad weather, are the only shopping and social centers. The island has no bars, no golf courses, no swimming pools. It has a post office, a community hall, and a ballfield where islanders leave the bats lying near home plate between games. Serious medical cases must be transported by helicopter to Crisfield or Salisbury. Young children attend island schools, but older ones travel daily by school boat to Crisfield High School, crossing many a rough water in the winter. The island is flooded so frequently that gravesites in the cemeteries have cement slabs on them to prevent the coffins from rising.

Smith Islanders have lived so close together throughout their history that they have learned to be very tolerant and accepting of behavior, although they are naturally suspicious of or uncomfortable with outsiders, especially someone who asks too many questions. They tend to assume first that any such person is an agent from the Internal Revenue Service sent to check on the watermen, who conduct most of their business in cash. To protect their privacy, they have made an art form of vagueness. Ask a native of the island the name of the person who owns a particular piece of land and he is liable to scratch his forehead and say he wished he knew. Islanders who work in the grocery stores and the post office, the crossroads of island traffic, are as mum as the island is flat about internal affairs. Their professed ignorance shields an effective, if mysterious, communications network. Any time police or DNR officials leave Crisfield to come to Smith Island, their arrival is always known in advance. Government officials as a species are generally regarded as dumber than clams. ''An islander can live by hisself,'' says Gerald Tyler. ''He's not raised to be dependent on the government, the state, or the county. I was raised to do for myself.''

Their distrust of outsiders and outside institutions historically has included banks. Many islanders reportedly keep their money in their

mattresses, or in safes, and some even bury it. Mainland bankers used to claim they could always tell when there had been a flood tide on the island, because they would suddenly receive an influx of wet paper money, brought over on one of the boats by a gun-toting islander, to be exchanged for dry bills.

While the islanders may eschew earthly forms of government, they embrace the kingdom of heaven. They attend one of the island's three Methodist churches regularly through the week, as often as three times on Sunday. An open Bible is more common than a newspaper in their homes. Says Tyler, "On Sundays, when everybody's dressed up and going to church, they seem so relaxed. They've done their work with the Lord's help. They're going to thank God for allowing them to make their living out of the water. If he wouldn't provide for us, we couldn't do it."

(As further testimony to their belief in the power of faith, stories of salvation and healing are not uncommon. Elmer Evans, treasurer of the Ewell Methodist Church for the past thirteen years, was a waterman until his knees and back gave out. Two operations failed, and he seemed doomed to live out his days in crippling pain. He attended a prayer meeting one night at the community hall. "You would not believe it," he recalls, "but an evangelist touched my leg, and it grew the same length as my other leg, right there in the meeting, with everyone watching. The evangelist asked me to stand up and touch my toes, and I could. And I can now, too.")

About the only form of authority the islanders appear to trust are the minister and the lay leaders of the churches. The island pastor, Kenneth Evans, presides over each of the three Sunday services, riding a circuit from Ewell to Tylerton. Each Wednesday night, lay leaders hold forth in the churches and, wielding power second only to that of the minister, are authorized to make decisions about church finances and policy.

Independent, autonomous, idiosyncratic, Smith Islanders might dispute the contention that they are like other people, or ever have been. As Tyler says, "The way we do things—we think different, not like people away from here. We listen to the weather report every day, but we don't pay any attention. We know what it's going to be. We can look around—at the sky, the stars, the wind, the way the birds act—and tell what it's going to be. Hurricanes come, and they tell us to get off the island, but if the signs look OK, we don't leave. I can't explain it. It's just a way of life, handed down from father to father."

The island has its share of modern-day problems, some of them peculiar to island living; others, to modern America. Kids drop out of school to work on the water. Alcoholism and drug trafficking are major problems. The islanders tend to be contrasted with watermen from Tangier Island, five miles to the south, whose workboats reputedly look

Smith Island

cleaner and are better kept. And then there is the inconvenience of the island's generator giving out from time to time, and the wells going bad with high bacteria counts.

The most significant problem has been a steady deterioration in the islanders' future as commercial fishermen because of the pollution of the Bay. Only the crab survives in any number, and it is being harvested in such record amounts that watermen and environmentalists alike wonder how much longer this can go on. The prospect of a single-product seafood industry is ominous, especially since more and more fishermen are turning to crabbing, which increases competition among the watermen and pressure on the crabs. Some nonislanders have suggested, with varying degrees of seriousness, that if fishing does give out, Smith Island should be turned into a tourist resort, or a retirement community, or an amusement park, or a center for marine research, or a military target similar to Bloodsworth Island, farther north.

Another problem in the eyes of the islanders is that outsiders have been moving onto the island for several years now. According to records in the county assessment office, the number of houses sold to outsiders has increased from two in 1983–84 to five in 1986, about ten percent

Smith Island

Smith Island

of the total number of land transfers in a year. While the numbers
hardly constitute a full-scale invasion, in the islander's view of things,
it amounts to "selling right and left to strangers." Even selling right and
left hasn't stabilized the island's population. Over the sixty years from
1920 to 1980, census figures show the population eroded from 770 to
606. The current estimate is 544. Despite these comings and goings,
most islanders resist any talk about moving away. Enos Evans, a retired
state government official who commuted to Annapolis and returned
home on weekends rather than give up living on Smith, says, "My
wife's been sexton of the church for thirty years, and now my
daughter's taking it over. I was born here. My parents are buried
here. Somebody has to be here to put flowers on their graves."

Yet another form of stress is at work on the island. First settled
for its grazing lands, the island has lost its grasslands to the rising sea.
The normal life of a marsh is a continuous cycle of erosion and buildup.
Building houses on marsh is like building on a sponge. One abandoned
Smith Island house has a piano in the living room, and that side of the

Overleaf: *Smith Island*

house has begun to sink slowly into the marsh. Some islanders suggest that if Sanford Justice were to develop his land, he would have to drive piling all the way to Hong Kong.

Tyler attributes much of the erosion to wave action caused by ships traveling too fast in the main channel of the Bay. "Six years ago, we could play ball in my backyard in Tylerton. Now, about fifteen to eighteen feet of ground is gone, and an average northeast tide floods my backyard with eight to ten inches of water."

Smith Island may disappear in the wake of a hurricane like Agnes in 1972, which scientists estimate dumped as much sediment into the Bay in five days as normally enters in 200 years. The flow of the Susquehanna was 1,000 times normal for a few days. Some estimate that sea level will rise five feet over the next century, enough to inundate almost all of the island. From the air, the island is a green ribbon shredded into bits and pieces by the water.

While the laws governing the natural selection of islands may be immutable, they are not taken as a foregone conclusion in the many places along the Atlantic seaboard where erosion threatens beachhead. It is one of the ironies in the conflict between environmentalists and developers that islands with money are the ones that protect themselves best against erosion. When land is highly valued—as it is at Ocean City, where it fetches a million dollars and more per acre—people fight to save their investments. They raise money to pump in sand and bulkhead the land. In other words, developers and affluent people—the kind with sailing boats and weekend condominiums along the Bay, the kind who have developed places like Annapolis and Kent Island—may be those best able to save Smith Island.

Aboard *The Pleiades II*, approaching Pocomoke and lunchtime, Tom Horton moved on to the subject of Smith Island and the criticism that he had tried to exploit the Justice issue in his article by neglecting to interview islanders and concentrating instead on those who supported his own concerns, a tactic that his opponents say is quite common among environmentalists.

"It would have been a better story," Horton halfway conceded, "if it had had more quotes by islanders. But the people of Smith Island will get a hearing. All good environmentalists get hysterical on the proper occasion. Our legitimate interest is to be concerned, involved. What are environmentalists going to fight on Smith Island? There is no wetlands involved."

Horton considered his own question for a minute, thinking about the watermen and what the future might hold for them. "Smith Island has to have options for its future," he said finally. "The state can't lock it up. I wish the state would broaden its consideration of what might be the proper role of the island.

"There are some, but not many, watermen who have a broad view of the Bay. I have a friend, a good friend, who is a skipjack captain. He believes in strong enforcement, but he will also scoop up every other oyster he can get as soon as the law isn't around. Watermen survive by being opportunists, just like the critters they hunt. They survive by fishing the hell out of the water and by being adept at switching off to other resources. It's the emotional versus the real. Watermen are always claiming the state wants to drive them out of business. Officially, the state wants to preserve watermen. They're a great symbol—eat an oyster caught in a sailboat by watermen living in cute towns. But watermen are the crux of a problem, and they don't realize the problem is not just the fish.''

He reflected further as the boat began to ease up to a dock. In the cabin below, First Mate Elizabeth had spread a table with fried chicken, potato salad, and fresh tomatoes. ''I shuttle back and forth in my mind from one extreme to the other, from twenty-eight acres of wetlands in Crisfield to Africa to famine. I look from the space shuttle one day, from Crisfield and Smith Island the next. Fifty percent of the planet lives on five percent of the earth. During the oyster season, watermen from all over the Bay congregate increasingly in a small number of areas. It reminds me of a column I once wrote on a theory from an essay, ''The Tragedy of the Commons,'' written about twenty years ago by a genetic biologist named Garrett Hardin. Its challenges reach far beyond Crisfield and Smith Island and watermen, and have never been faced squarely by society.

''Professor Hardin tells the parable of a pasture (translate Bay for our purposes) open to all. Each herdsman (waterman, if you wish) will reasonably try to keep as many cattle as he can on the commons. . . . As population increases, the pressure on the commons consequently begins to rise, and each herdsman rationally asks what he gains by putting one more head of cattle there. The answer is that it is in his interest to do so, because he gets virtually all the gain from selling an extra cow, whereas the loss resulting from overgrazing is shared among all the users. The rational herdsman concludes that the only sensible course for him to pursue is to add another animal to his herd, and another . . . but this is the conclusion reached by each and every rational herdsman sharing a commons. Therein is the tragedy. Each man is locked into a system that compels him to increase his herd without limit—in a world that is limited.

''It's hard to swing people away from a growth economy,'' Horton said as the boat came to rest at the dock. ''The whole current system is tied to a tax base. ''If you want to increase the tax base, you have to develop land. Taxwise, the best thing for Somerset County would be a nuclear power plant. It has a monstrous tax base and doesn't add lots of people to the town. Perhaps, in thinking how to make Somerset more developed, we need ideas from nontraditional developers. Perhaps, as I once suggested, we should pay Crisfield for being Crisfield, remaining

Overleaf: *Bridge at South River, Annapolis*

undeveloped, a place that others in the state can enjoy but should also support. But, in the absence of these things, you have to deal with growth as best you can.

"The ultimate quest is in man's being able to reconcile himself with nature. How can more and more of us live on the same resources without degrading them? It's not enough just to control sewage, sediment, and fertilizer runoff if millions more people are coming in. Pollution regulations don't regulate people and growth. In the long run, the American philosophy of 'grow or die' is very destructive."

Epilogue

The Crisfield Maritime Park Plan isn't dead, just very moribund. Occasionally, *The Crisfield Times* urges the leaders of the community to present the plan again, but there doesn't seem to be any news of enough significance to overcome the inertia of doing so. In the meantime, plans to attract more tourists move ahead in tiny increments —a new fishing tournament is to be held in Crisfield; a new hotel is under construction; an old one is being renovated. The town's two motels seem a little busier than normal, and its three major boat dealers are reporting good sales.

Sanford Justice rearranged his timetable for presenting his plan to the Somerset County Zoning Board, aiming for late fall of 1986. But complications in putting together the different components delayed the plan further, and he put it off indefinitely, confirming the opinions of those who had predicted nothing would come of it. But something has already come of it—Smith Island has become another battleground in the Chesapeake region between developer and environmentalist, between forces of change and protectors and preservers of the status quo.

Bibliography

Books

Bakeless, John. *The Eyes of Discovery.* Philadelphia: Lippincott, 1950.

Barbour, Philip L. *The Three Worlds of Captain John Smith.* Boston: Houghton Mifflin, 1964.

Blair, Carvel Hall, and Willits Dyer Ansel. *Chesapeake Bay Notes and Sketches.* Cambridge, MD: Tidewater Publishers, 1970.

Buchanan, George. *The Boat Repair Manual.* New York: Arco, 1985.

Burgess, Robert H. *Chesapeake Sailing Craft,* Part 1. Cambridge, MD: Tidewater Publishers, 1975.

Earle, Swepson. *Chesapeake Bay Country.* Baltimore: Thomsen-Ellis, 1929.

Fisher, M.F.K. *Consider the Oyster.* New York: Duell, Sloan and Pearce, 1941.

Footner, Hulbert. *Rivers of the Eastern Shore.* New York: Farrar & Rinehart, 1944.

Hall, S. Warren, III. *Tangier Island.* Philadelphia: University of Pennsylvania, 1939.

Hedeen, Robert A. *Naturalist on the Nanticoke.* Centreville, MD: Tidewater Publishers, 1982.

Hill, Norman Alan, ed. Malcolm Westcott Hill, J. Hooper Edmondson, and F.R. Vernon Williams, assoc. eds. *Chesapeake Cruise.* Baltimore: George W. King Printing Co., 1944.

Klingel, Gilbert C. *The Bay.* Baltimore: Johns Hopkins, 1951.

Lippson, Alice Jane, and Robert L. Lippson. *Life in the Chesapeake Bay.* Baltimore: Johns Hopkins, 1984.

Marvil, James E., M.D. *Sailing Rams.* Lewes, DE: Sussex Press, 1974.

Middleton, Arthur Pierce. *Tobacco Coast.* Newport News, VA: The Mariners' Museum, 1953.

Morison, Samuel Eliot. *The Oxford History of the American People.* Vol. 1. New York: New American Library, 1972.

Norden, Arnold W., Donald C. Forester, and George H. Fenwick, eds. *Threatened and Endangered Plants and Animals of Maryland.* Annapolis: Maryland Department of Natural Resources, 1984.

Payson, Harold H. *Go Build Your Own Boat!* New York: Van Nostrand Reinhold, 1983.

Peffer, Randall S. *Watermen.* Baltimore: Johns Hopkins, 1979.

Rouse, Parke, Jr. *Roll, Chesapeake Roll.* Chesapeake, VA: Norfolk County Historical Society, 1972.

Rukert, Norman G. *The Port: Pride of Baltimore.* Baltimore: Bodine & Assoc., 1982.

Schubel, J.R. *The Living Chesapeake.* Baltimore: Johns Hopkins, 1981.

Semmes, Raphael. *Captains and Mariners of Early Maryland.* Baltimore: Johns Hopkins, 1937.

Teal, John, and Mildred Teal. *Life and Death of the Salt Marsh.* New York: Ballantine Books, 1969.

Wilson, Woodrow T., *History of Crisfield and Surrounding Areas on Maryland's Eastern Shore.* Baltimore: Gateway Press, 1974.

Magazines and Newspapers

Baltimore Sun, Baltimore. "On Environment," biweekly columns by Tom Horton. 1984–86.

Chesapeake Bay Magazine, Annapolis, MD. 1986–87.

The Crisfield Times, Crisfield, MD. 1985–87.

Acknowledgments

I would like to thank the following people for their generous assistance: Frank and Joy Adams, Ron Adkins, Daniel Boone, Jamie Bradshaw, Marian Carson, Tim and Pat Carson, Mary Chandler, Rod Coggin, Jeff Crockett, Ruth Custis, Frank Dize, Eugene Evans, Ilia and Joseph Fehrer, Jimmy Goslee, John Goslee, Frank Hirst, Herbert and Imogene Horton, Tom Horton, Paul Jewel, Sanford Justice, Frances Kitching, Dick Landon, Grant Lawson, Becky Lowe, Wick Lowe, Fred Monk, John "Lank" Parks, Ron Purnell, Sandy Riggin, Jon Ritter, Gerald Tyler, Vincent Vita, Tom Ward, Elizabeth Warren, John Warren, Josephine Warren, John Page Williams, Lee and Leslie Wilson, Ellen Wollensack.

Special thanks to *The Philadelphia Inquirer Sunday Magazine* for allowing me to adapt part of an article for them on Smith Island to suit my purposes here. Laura Ritter, editor of *The Crisfield Times* when this book was written, wrote the original Smith Island article with me, and I am grateful for her research and guidance on the sections on Smith Island and Crisfield.